M000214291

HONOR

THE UNIVERSITY OF CHICAGO PRESS, CHICAGO 60637
THE UNIVERSITY OF CHICAGO PRESS, LTD., LONDON

© 1994 by The University of Chicago
All rights reserved. Published 1994
Printed in the United States of America

03   02   01   00   99   98   97   96   95   94   1   2   3   4   5

ISBN: 0-226-77407-4 (cloth)
0-226-77408-2 (paper)

Library of Congress Cataloging-in-Publication Data

Stewart, Frank Henderson.

Honor / Frank Henderson Stewart.

p.   cm.

Includes bibliographical references and index.

1. Bedouins.   2. Honor.   3. Arab countries—Social life and customs.   I. Title.

DS36.9.B4S765   1994

305.892'7—dc20   94-12515

CIP

⊚ The paper used in this publication meets the minimum requirements of the American
National Standard for Information Sciences—Permanence of Paper for Printed Library Materials,
ANSI Z39.48-1984.

HONOR

Frank Henderson Stewart

THE UNIVERSITY OF CHICAGO PRESS

Chicago & London

For Judy Blanc

"But the honour—the honour, monsieur! . . . The honour . . . that is real—that is!"

Joseph Conrad, *Lord Jim*

CONTENTS

PREFACE

In 1965 a well-known anthropologist, J. G. Peristiany, brought out the volume of essays by various hands entitled *Honour and Shame: The Values of Mediterranean Society*. Honor was evidently a subject whose time had come: the rate at which new publications on the topic appear has continued to increase ever since.[1] Nor is it only anthropologists who deal with honor: historians show a growing interest in the subject, and many of them refer with respect to the anthropological literature.[2] Indeed, anthropologists now seem to be considered *the* experts on the subject. Whether they deserve this status is not entirely clear. The anthropological literature on honor certainly has a number of curious features, one of them being that it rarely asks what exactly honor is. In this work I shall try to provide the outline of an answer to that question.

The essay falls into three main parts. The first (chapters 2 through 5) is mainly an analysis of the Western notion of honor as it has been since about the time of the Renaissance. The second (chapters 6 through 9) is mainly devoted to the Bedouin notion of '*ird*, a term usually (and I believe correctly) translated as 'honor'. The third (chapters 10 through 12) is mainly a comparison of the Western ideas with the Bedouin ones.

I have not attempted to provide either a comprehensive or a balanced discussion of honor. I have dealt at some length with topics about which I had something to say, while others, no less important, about which I had little or nothing to say, have been more or less neglected; hence, for instance, the brevity of chapter 10. Even the topics that are dealt with at some length deserve far more profound

---

1. Recent anthologies, primarily anthropological in nature, include Gilmore 1987a; Fiume 1989; Peristiany and Pitt-Rivers 1991a; and Gautheron 1991b. Pitarch 1984 is a collection of interviews on the subject of honor; the editor is (or then was) an officer in the Spanish army who holds a degree in law and who is also active as a journalist. He contributes two introductory essays to the book.
2. To mention just a few examples, see the references to honor in Farr 1988; Neuschel 1989; Stone 1990; and Treggiari 1991.

treatment than they receive here. Unfortunately, other commitments make it impossible for me to deal with honor more thoroughly, at least for the time being. I hope nevertheless that the reader will find in this work enough that is of interest to make up for its numerous shortcomings.

ACKNOWLEDGMENTS

Most of this essay was written while I was a fellow at the Annenberg Institute, Philadelphia, and a preliminary version of it was presented at a seminar there early in 1992. I should like to express my deep appreciation to everyone at the institute for providing an ideal environment for research. In particular, I should like to thank David Goldenberg, the Associate Director, for his unstinting support.

The Lucius N. Littauer Foundation awarded me a grant-in-aid while I was at the Annenberg Institute, and I am most grateful to the foundation's director, Bill Frost, for the personal interest that he has for so long taken in my work.

The following have been kind enough to read draft versions of this essay, and while they bear no responsibility for its contents, their extensive remarks have been invaluable to me: Talal Asad, Patricia Crone, Margaret Gilbert, Charles Jarrett, Etan Kohlberg, and Melveena McKendrick. I should also like to thank those who commented rather more briefly: Fredrik Barth, William Brinner, Esther Cohen, Michael Cook, Itamar Even-Zohar, David D. Gilmore, Ward Goodenough, Gerd Grasshoff, Charles Lindholm, Ann Elizabeth Mayer, Rodney Needham, Michael Singer, Patti Skigen, Guy Stroumsa, Sarah Stroumsa, Alan Watson, and Viola Winder.

My greatest debt is to Cindy Niedoroda, without whom this work would perhaps never have been written.

A NOTE ABOUT ARABIC

Each community in the Arab world speaks its own dialect, and the differences between the dialects of two regions very distant from each other may be so great that they are not mutually intelligible. Literary Arabic—the language of newspapers and magazines, of literature, of news broadcasts—is, in contrast, essentially the same throughout the Arab world, and is different from any dialect. Most of the Arabic words that appear in this book are used both in the literary language and in many of the dialects. In order to simplify comparison, I have generally employed the literary, rather than the dialectal, form of all words (apart from proper names) for which there is a literary equivalent. Thus ʿird ('honor') is a simplified transcription of the word as it occurs in literary Arabic (ʿirḍ); in the dialect of the Bedouin of central Sinai among whom I did fieldwork the word is pronounced ʿarḍ.

The fact that a word is used both in literary Arabic and in many dialects does not entail that it has the same meaning throughout; its meaning may vary not only as between the literary language and the dialects but also from one dialect to another.

The use among the Bedouin of central Sinai of most of the Arabic terms that appear in this book can be illustrated from Stewart 1988–90. This is a collection of sixty-nine texts, each of which is given in English translation (vol. 1) and in the original Arabic (vol. 2). Five of the texts are written, the rest are oral. All the written texts, and all but one of the oral texts, were produced in the ordinary course of affairs, that is, when the Bedouin were talking to each other (and not to me), or when they were writing something down for their own purposes (and not at my instigation). The second volume contains an Arabic-English glossary. In what follows, page references to this glossary are given on the first occurrence of certain Arabic terms that appear in it. This will enable even non-Arabists to form some idea of how a given term is used in central Sinai. For ʿarḍ, see Stewart 1988–90, 2:199 (where the reference "42.2" should be deleted).

1

METHOD

If we are to judge by the citations to be found in the works of the anthropologists, there is not a great deal to read about honor. Julian Pitt-Rivers, "perhaps the leading authority on honor,"[1] writes that before the social sciences recognized the existence of honor in the mid-1960s, "the little that was published on this subject was limited to studies of the history of the concept in literature and some tendentious articles in encyclopedias";[2] and there is nothing in the work of his colleagues that would indicate otherwise. But is it really so?

Even if we confine ourselves to the literature in European languages, the answer is clearly no. It does not matter, perhaps, that Pitt-Rivers makes no mention of the philosophical work on the subject, for most of it is not very distinguished.[3] And he can be forgiven for ignoring the compositions of the Italian honor theorists of the sixteenth century, which he may view as outdated.[4] But there is also an immense juristic literature on honor, and to overlook this is inexcusable, not only because it is so voluminous, but also because it is so good. Indeed, the most intensive and sophisticated discussion of honor in any European language is probably to be found in the writings of the German lawyers during the nineteenth and twentieth centuries.[5]

Yet though far more work has been done on honor than the anthro-

1. Hahn 1984, 149; I think that Hahn, who is an historian, expresses a widely held opinion, and for this reason, among others, what Pitt-Rivers has to say about honor will be given special attention in the pages that follow.
2. Pitt-Rivers 1991, 20–21. Unless otherwise indicated, all translations from foreign languages are my own.
3. See, for instance, Jeudon 1911; Terraillon 1912; Reiner 1956; and Bollnow 1962, 47–61. For further references, see Hirsch 1967, 7–12.
4. Erspamer 1982 offers a good bibliography; see also Bryson 1935.
5. For bibliographies, see Hirsch 1967 and Tenckhoff 1974. The modern German juristic literature on the subject is usually reckoned to have begun with the first edition of Adolph Dietrich Weber's treatise (1793–94; not seen by me). The juristic literature in languages other than German is also very substantial: for instance, the bibliography attached to Vescovi 1902–6, which lists mainly Italian works published in the nineteenth century, contains over three hundred entries.

pologists seem to realize, it would be wrong to pretend that the subject is in anything but a primitive state of development. The analytic literature on honor (apart from the work of the jurists) is limited and mostly unimpressive, while the descriptive studies, though often very good, cover only a small part of the ground. The history of honor has not been traced in any detail for even one of the major languages, or the major countries, of Europe; the subject lies in a vast twilight, broken only by a few bright, but narrow, beams of light.

In these circumstances it is not surprising that comparative work on honor has scarcely begun. We know, for instance, that 'face' is important in China,[6] and we are told that "honor (*meiyo;* literally 'glory of the name') [is] a fundamental concept which has regulated Japanese society in various ways since ancient times."[7] But little has been done to bring such East Asian notions into a clear relationship with the more familiar ideas of Western Asia and of Europe.[8] And there is an even more obvious deficiency in the anthropological literature. A large part of it, both ethnographic and theoretical, deals with honor among the peoples of southern Europe; but anthropologists have not made any serious attempt to compare southern European honor with honor among the peoples of northern Europe, even though honor was of great importance in the Germanic world and is the subject of an extensive literature.[9] My ignorance of the relevant languages has prevented me from reading the Far Eastern sources, but in what follows I shall make some use of that part of the northern European literature that is written in English or in German.

Modern descriptive studies of honor can be divided into two classes, the field studies and the armchair studies. *Field studies* are those based on information that the author collected at first hand from the subjects; the rest are *armchair studies.* In principle both approaches can be used in a single work, but in practice there is little overlap between the two types. The armchair studies are almost always based on texts produced by the people whose concept of honor is under investigation:

6. Hu 1944 (an invaluable study).

7. Saitō 1983. For a different kind of Japanese honor, see Saikaku 1981.

8. Asano-Tamanoi 1987 is one of the few exceptions, at any rate in Western languages; there may well be publications in Far Eastern languages of which I am not aware.

9. For bibliographies, see Korff 1966; Zunkel 1975; and Frevert 1991.

medieval Spanish laws,[10] French Arthurian epics,[11] Icelandic sagas,[12] treatises on ethics from the Spain of Phillip II,[13] seventeenth-century English dramas,[14] eighteenth-century court martial records,[15] or whatever. These studies usually allow us a high degree of control over the author's work; provided that the original texts survive, we can, if we are ready to take the trouble, distinguish clearly between the author's ideas and those of the subjects as they appear in the texts. Almost all armchair studies give exact references to their sources, and many of them also quote those sources extensively.[16]

Field studies can also employ texts produced by the subjects: Tore Nordenstam, for instance, in his book *Sudanese Ethics* (1968), bases his discussion of honor on interviews (in English) with Sudanese Arab students. These interviews were recorded on tape, transcribed, and published in his book. Like all texts, these have their limitations and must be treated critically; but they allow us at least to hear the voice of the Sudanese themselves, even if they are speaking to a foreigner in a foreign language.

Nordenstam is a philosopher, not an anthropologist. Anthropologists usually go about their work in a very different way. When they produce descriptive studies of honor, they deal mostly in generalizations, and tend to present their conclusions without giving any very clear idea of the evidence from which they were derived. Verbatim quotations from the subjects, in the subjects' own language, are few, and examples of honor in action—for honor is a matter of deeds, not just of words—are no more common.[17] Pitt-Rivers' descriptive work

10. Serra Ruiz 1969.
11. Robreau 1981.
12. Gehl 1937 is still the fullest study; references to more recent publications are given in Bauman 1986, 148 n. 5, to which add Vermeyden 1990. The Icelandic sagas are of the greatest importance to students of honor, but my ignorance of Old Norse has prevented me from making much use of them. See further appendix 2 below.
13. Chauchadis 1984.
14. Barber 1957.
15. Gilbert 1976.
16. Though often, alas, without translation. Not everyone who is interested in honor can be assumed to know Old French or Middle High German.
17. Steul 1981, a study of the Pashtun code of honor, which contains details of over a hundred disputes, is a laudable exception; but even this study does not entirely meet the mark, since the accounts of the disputes, valuable though they are, are not properly linked to the author's analysis of the meaning and use of the various Pashto words that relate to honor.

on honor in an Andalusian village is an early example of this method; his approach was adopted later by many others. One of the main drawbacks of this method is that it makes it difficult or even impossible to distinguish between the author's own ideas and those of his subjects. In general it is evident, despite their discreet silence on the subject, that the field studies are based on rather small amounts of information, and the difference in this respect between them and the more extensive of the armchair studies can hardly be exaggerated. Barber 1957, perhaps the most remarkable of all the armchair studies, is based on analyses of over five thousand occurrences of the noun 'honor' in the English drama of the late sixteenth and the seventeenth century;[18] and while this is an exceptionally large body of material, works such as Farès 1932, Gehl 1937, and Robreau 1981 deal at least with hundreds of examples. The armchair studies also on occasion deal with large quantities of case material: one scholar analyzed about a thousand disputes involving honor that were tried between the sixteenth and the nineteenth century in the Basque province of Vizcaya,[19] while another dealt with some 340 prosecutions for insult in the district of Andernach (West Germany) during the years 1950–60.[20]

It is perhaps worth thinking for a moment about what would be involved in a reasonably thorough descriptive study of the notion of honor in our own society.[21] I suppose we would expect its author to understand all the subtleties of the English language, to make extensive use of written materials (notably newspapers and popular fiction), to monitor radio and television broadcasts, to distribute questionnaires, and to record what people say when they talk (preferably not only in interviews) about honor. An anthropologist working in an alien culture is, of course, limited in many ways; but we should beware of lowering our standards simply because the culture being described is not our own. We may have to be content, faute de mieux, with superficial

18. Barber 1985, 149 n. 18.
19. Martín Rodríguez 1973, 4.
20. Fleskes 1965, 19–20. Fleskes also talked to some of the officials involved in these prosecutions, so that his work is also in part a field study.
21. The only systematic empirical studies that I know of concerning ideas of honor in a contemporary Western society are Lévy, Muxel, and Percheron 1991 (an interesting and imaginative investigation that is based on questionnaires distributed to a sample of some 1,400 French students aged fourteen through twenty as well as on essays that the students wrote) and Gautheron 1991a (a brief study based on a sample of ninety schoolchildren).

or dubious information, but we should at least not delude ourselves into believing that it is adequate or reliable.

This essay, to the extent that it is descriptive, is a field study, or rather a preliminary report on a field study. Bedouin honor is a complex topic, and not every aspect of it is discussed here. I hope to deal with the subject more fully in a two-volume account of Sinai Bedouin law currently in preparation.[22] In that same work there will also be an account of how the data were collected. It is intended that all the materials on which this ethnographic work is based—field notes, tape recordings, genealogies, census records and so on—will eventually be made available to those who wish to consult them. Some of what is asserted in the present essay can already be checked against a body of texts produced by the Bedouin themselves and published in Stewart 1988–90. In that same book will be found references to a few other texts that were published in articles.

Most descriptive studies of honor—whether the author worked in an armchair or in the field—can be classed as either lexical or conceptual. The *lexical* approach is to study the use of one or more words in the language of the people whose notions of honor are being investigated. Barber (1957) confines himself to a single noun, but most authors, like Hu (1944), Herzfeld (1980), Robreau (1981), and Martin (1984), investigate a small number of closely related terms. The *conceptual* approach is to start from some general idea of what honor is, and then to examine its particular features in a certain society. Gehl 1937, Jones 1959, and Abu-Lughod 1986 are examples of this method. Now the author of a lexical study may claim with some plausibility that her work can be done without worrying too much about the notion of honor in general.[23] But when the author of a conceptual study fails to offer a definition of "this most elusive of social concepts,"[24] then the result is apt to be a certain lack of focus. It may not be clear why some things count as honor and others do not, why certain things are grouped together and others excluded from the grouping. Neither Gehl nor Jones explains what he means by honor, and the work of the latter in particular suffers as a result. Abu-Lughod, in contrast, does offer something like a definition, if not of 'honor', at any rate of 'code

22. Cf. Stewart 1988–90, 1:xi.
23. Thus Robreau 1981, 1–4.
24. Patterson 1982, 80.

of honor'. She writes that "the ideals or moral virtues of Bedouin society together constitute what I refer to as the Bedouin code of honor."[25]
But this in turn raises new questions; for instance, do the ideals or
moral virtues of every society constitute a code of honor, or is there
something special about Bedouin ideals or moral virtues that makes
them a code of honor? And if there is, what is it?

In the descriptive part of this book I shall use a mainly lexical approach; but since this is primarily a comparative (or analytic) study, I
begin with a sketch—and it will soon be evident that it is no more than
a sketch—of a concept of honor that can be applied cross-culturally.

25. Abu-Lughod 1986, 86, though cf. 45.

PART ONE

2

THE NATURE OF HONOR

When an anthropologist or historian identifies something in a non-Western society as honor, the meaning is simply that the thing so identified is more or less the same as what is called 'honor' in ordinary English (or *Ehre* in ordinary German, or *chest'* in ordinary Russian, etc.).[1] In other words, the common Western notion of honor is applied cross-culturally. I believe that this practice is not misconceived; for instance, as I have already indicated, I think that scholars have been justified in translating the Arabic word '*ird* as 'honor'. But the Western notion of honor has never been analyzed in a satisfactory fashion, so that when we say, for instance, that '*ird* means 'honor', it is still far from clear exactly what '*ird* is.[2] I therefore begin with a brief analysis of the Western concept of honor, or at any rate of part of it. Since honor no longer plays much part in our thinking, I shall draw my illustrative material mostly from the past. But the past in question is fairly recent, and its ideas about honor are quite familiar to us.

Most of us, I suspect, feel that a single thing is being referred to in such phrases as the following: "men and women [. . .] with high standards of honor and duty,"[3] "an attack of outraged honour,"[4] "under the obligation of honour,"[5] and "we have satisfied our hon-

---

1. The words used for honor in the various major modern European languages are of course not *exact* synonyms of each other; but they are very close to each other in meaning, and all stand in marked contrast, for instance, to '*ird* as it is used by the Bedouin (see further the last part of chapter 12).

2. Thus Herzfeld (1985, 289), who rejects the usual translation of the Greek *filotimo* as 'honor', remarks wisely that "in general, monolithic 'translations' of indigenous moral terms, while perhaps acceptable for the sake of convenience in a fully documented ethnography, become dangerously counterproductive when they are used as the basis of comparative analyses."

3. Kennan 1891, 1:186.

4. Braine 1968, 65. Braine is unusual among modern English novelists in that the notion of honor is evidently important to him; the word appears many times in this work.

5. Marston 1973, 41, quoting a letter from the year 1642.

our."[6] I believe that a single underlying idea is indeed involved in all these cases. But this is a case that needs to be argued. For certainly when one looks at the way the word 'honor' is used, one finds it referring to things apparently quite different from each other. Let me illustrate this with a couple of examples from the Sherlock Holmes stories.

The first one comes from *The Naval Treaty*.[7] A copy of a secret treaty between England and Italy is stolen from the desk of Percy Phelps, an official at the Foreign Office. He says, "I turn to you Mr. Holmes, as absolutely my last hope. If you fail me, then my honour as well as my position are forever forfeited." Subsequently, something occurs which leads Phelps to suspect that an attempt may have been made on his life. He says to Holmes, "I begin to believe that I am the unconscious centre of some monstrous conspiracy, and that my life is aimed at as well as my honour." Towards the end of the tale, when Holmes has recovered the lost document, Phelps says to him, "You have saved my honour."

Why is Phelps's honor in danger? There is little in the story to suggest that he may be suspected of having acted dishonestly, but the circumstances under which the theft occurred were such that an accusation of negligence against Phelps would not be entirely absurd. It seems that if the document is not recovered, then he will be seen as having betrayed a trust in that he was negligent when it was his duty to act with the utmost care. But even if he was negligent, his having been so does not entail the loss of his honor: for if he was negligent, then he was negligent irrespective of whether the treaty is recovered. What determines whether Phelps retains his honor is evidently not what kind of person he is, or what he did or failed to do. The honor that Phelps fears that he will lose is something outside himself, something, it might seem, in the attitude of others towards him, or in what they believe about him.

Consider now another Holmes story, *The Adventure of the Three Garridebs*.[8] A reclusive old man, Mr. Nathan Garrideb, is visited by an American who represents himself as one John Garrideb, a person Nathan has never heard of. The American relates an extraordinary tale

---

6. From Rudyard Kipling's story *Judson and the Empire*. It was first published in 1893, and appears in the volume *Many Inventions*.

7. The story, which was first published in 1893, appears in *Memoirs of Sherlock Holmes* by Arthur Conan Doyle.

8. The story, which was first published in 1924, appears in *The Case Book of Sherlock Holmes* by Arthur Conan Doyle.

to the old man, the essence of which is that if the two of them can find a third person by the name of Garrideb, then they will all three share in a large fortune. Nathan writes to Holmes seeking his help. The American—who is of course a crook—learns of this and, much perturbed, himself goes to see Holmes, evidently in order to find out what Holmes intends to do. Later the same day Holmes visits Nathan, and the following dialogue occurs (the first speaker is Holmes, the second Nathan):

> "Did he [the American] tell you of our interview today?"
> "Yes, he came straight back to me. He had been very angry."
> "Why should he be angry?"
> "He seemed to think it was some reflection on his honour. But he was quite cheerful again when he returned."

What the American seemed to think was a reflection on his honor was the letter that the old man wrote to Holmes. The American at first feared that Nathan was suspicious of his story and had asked Holmes to investigate it. In the interview with the American, Holmes had indicated to him that this was not in fact the case, that Nathan had merely asked him to track down a third Garrideb, and so the American was quite cheerful when he returned to Nathan.

The kind of honor referred to here looks quite different from Phelps's honor. Phelps's honor lay outside Phelps, it seemed to be something to do with how others viewed him. The American's honor, in contrast, is closely tied to him; apparently it is something like his integrity or his veracity or his moral character. Just how intimately this kind of honor is identified with its bearer can be seen from another passage in the story. During their interview, the American tells Holmes that he feels bad about the fact that Nathan got in touch with Holmes. In response, Holmes reassures the American about the contents of Nathan's letter. He says, "There was no reflection upon you." This evidently means much the same as if Holmes had said, "There was no reflection upon your honour."

The contrast between the two examples appears very clearly if we consider some of the words that might be substituted for 'honor' in its various occurrences while still producing sentences that are consistent with their context. In the examples from *The Naval Treaty,* one could replace 'honor' with, for instance, 'good name' or 'reputation'. In the Garrideb example, one could replace it with, for instance, 'integrity' or 'veracity' or 'character'. Words like these could not replace 'honor' in the *Naval Treaty* examples; if Phelps is a man of integrity, then he remains one irrespective of whether the treaty is ever recovered. It would be less obviously odd to replace 'honor' in the Garrideb example with a word like 'reputation' or 'good name'. Yet it would also be strange, in that it is common knowledge[9] between the two men that John Garrideb is not someone well known, and in particular that Nathan has never heard of him. Nor I think could one make good sense of, for instance, "he seemed to think it was some reflection on his good name" by bringing in the fact that Nathan has (as he thinks the American believes) written to Holmes asking Holmes to investigate the truth of the American's story; the sentence with 'good name' in it seems, as I have suggested, to imply a preexisting good reputation that is known to both parties, and not to refer to a reputation that is about to be created. In any case, we can easily imagine Nathan, without bringing any third party into the picture, showing to the American in some unmistakable way that he suspects him of being an impostor; and the American could equally well take this to be a reflection on his honor.

Many analyses of honor view it as having two main aspects, one being Phelps's kind of honor, which is *outer* or *external*, the other being the American's kind, which is *inner* or *internal*.[10] Now how are these two aspects related? One possibility is that they are only remotely or loosely related. But most people who have dealt with these matters seem to have felt intuitively (as I do myself) that the relationship is a close one. Indeed, it has seemed proper to see honor precisely as a single thing with different 'aspects', one of which is involved in Phelps's case and the other in the American's. Given this widespread feeling, an analysis that does not connect the two aspects of honor closely to each other starts life with a marked handicap.

The two-aspect analyses of honor are not the only ones. There are accounts that view honor as having only a single aspect: one anthropologist says that the word "might best be translated as esteem, respect,

9. For a recent analysis of this notion, see Gilbert 1992.

10. These terms are the ones normally used in the German literature. In English there are no standard terms, so that Curtis Watson, for instance, refers to these as "honor in its public sense" and "honor in its private sense" (1960, 136), and Jones (1959, 151) sometimes writes of the "subjective and objective meanings" of honor. The distinction was already made in the sixteenth century; see, for instance, Landi 1695, 1:182–83 (first published in 1564).

prestige, or some combination of these attributes, depending on local usage,"[11] another writes that "a man's honour may be defined as the moral worth he possesses in the eyes of the society of which he is a member,"[12] while a sociologist sees it as "a culturally instilled conception of self as sacred social object."[13] And the best-known definition by an anthropologist, that of Julian Pitt-Rivers, offers an analysis in terms of what he calls three facets: "a sentiment, a manifestation of this sentiment in conduct, and the evaluation of this conduct by others."[14] Most analysts, however, have believed that the concept has two aspects, or at any rate two main aspects. In fact Pitt-Rivers himself offered a two-aspect account before he offered the three-facet account: "Honour is the value of a person in his own eyes, but also in the eyes of his society. It is his estimation of his own worth, his *claim* to pride, but it is also the acknowledgement of that claim, his excellence recognised by society, his *right* to pride."[15] Pitt-Rivers' most recent attempt to characterize honor seems also to be in terms of two aspects: honor, he writes, is "at once a sentiment and an objective social fact; on the one hand, a moral state [. . .] and at the same time a means of representing the moral worth of others."[16]

In the next two sections I shall consider in some detail one or two of the more important analyses of honor, and in the section that follows I shall present what I believe to be the correct theory.

The only major philosopher of recent times to have given much thought to honor is Schopenhauer, who devotes most of a chapter to the subject in his *Aphorismen zur Lebensweisheit*.[17] He wrote, no doubt

11. Brandes 1987, 121.
12. Westermarck 1912–17, 2:137. This is one of the earliest definitions offered by an anthropologist. A number of other analysts were at this time offering much the same definition of the term.
13. Flynn 1977, 49.
14. Pitt-Rivers 1968, 503. This definition has been particularly influential; a distinguished sociologist, for instance, writes that it expresses the "*communis opinio*" (Patterson 1982, 79).
15. Pitt-Rivers 1966, 22. Oddly enough, this passage is reproduced unchanged in Pitt-Rivers 1977, 1. Perhaps Pitt-Rivers, after a flirtation with the three-facet theory, decided that after all his original proposal was best.
16. Pitt-Rivers 1991, 21.
17. This work is part of the author's *Parerga und Paralipomena,* and was first published in 1851. There are several English translations (none of which I have referred to).

somewhat tongue in cheek, that "honor, taken objectively, is the opinion that others have of our value, and taken subjectively, our fear of that opinion."[18] Both parts of this definition fit well enough with Phelps's honor, but it is no help in understanding the American's.

In Schopenhauer's world, honor was more than just a matter of academic interest: in the nineteenth and early twentieth century, honor had an important place in German life, and certain offenses against honor are to this day recognized by the criminal law.[19] As has been mentioned, there is a large juristic literature on the subject. One interesting feature of this literature is that it has never even come close to its main objective, which is to produce a theory of honor that will make sense of the law and gain general acceptance.[20] Let us, simply by way of illustration, look at one of the many incompatible analyses that have been offered. It appears in the work of Moritz Liepmann, a professor of criminal law who was in his time—the early years of the twentieth century—the leading expert on insult. His problem (and that of his colleagues) is this. In German law it is a criminal offense for A to insult B, for example, by calling him a swine. Virtually all commentators agree that what is being defended by this law is B's honor.[21] But what precisely is honor? It is not something universally distributed that protects everybody from being called a swine—if B is truly porcine, then A is within his rights in calling him a swine.[22] The law defends only

---

Though there is no standard pagination, the passages referred to here can easily be traced, since they all come from chapter 4 of the *Aphorismen*.

18. Schopenhauer n.d., 58.

19. A good many such offenses come to court. In the 1960s the number of convictions under § 185 of the criminal code, which deals with insults, was between eight and ten thousand a year; at the beginning of the century it was more than fifty thousand a year (Simson and Geerds 1969, 300). For criminological analyses of such cases, see Fleskes 1965 and Christiansen 1965 (I have not myself seen Christiansen's work).

20. This is frequently bemoaned by the jurists, e.g., Hirsch 1967, 5 n. 16 (*bellum omnium contra omnes*); Brezina 1987, 11 (*geradezu babylonische Begriffswirrung*). Similarly, Tenckhoff 1974, 14.

21. Some early theories that connected this law with something other than honor are surveyed in Tenckhoff 1974, 16–25.

22. This, at any rate, is the general view, though there are one or two jurists who disagree. It has been observed that, broadly speaking, in the law of the countries of Central Europe, if the statement that one makes is true, then it is not punishable as an offense against honor; whereas in the Latin countries (e.g., Spain and Italy) the fact that the statement is true is not in itself a sufficient defense (Berdugo Gómez de la Torre 1987,

honorable people. Now Liepmann defines honor as "the possession of certain qualities, specifically those qualities that determine a person's worth."[23] Liepmann observed, of course, that if (as his definition implies) honor is a true personal quality[24] (like integrity, for instance, or strength, or courage), then B is just as honorable after he has been called a swine as he was before; so his honor has not been damaged, and unless we can find some other interest of B's that *has* been injured, A has committed no offense against him. Liepmann therefore derives from the basic notion of honor two new notions of honor, both of which represent interests that the law *can* protect. One is "objectified honor," which is a person's good reputation, the other "subjectified honor," a person's sense of their own worth.[25] When A falsely calls B a thief, before witnesses, it is B's objectified honor that is impugned (though his subjectified honor may also be affected); when A calls B a swine in private, it is only B's subjectified honor that is harmed.[26]

This ingenious analysis can deal with both our Sherlock Holmes examples. Liepmann would claim that when Phelps says "my honor"

---

73). See further the useful comparative and historical discussion of this topic in Kohler 1900, 119–39.

23. *Wir verstehen unter Ehre zunächst den Besitz bestimmter Eigenschaften. Und zwar sind es diejenigen Eigenschaften, die den Wert eines Menschen bestimmen* (Liepmann 1909, 12). Elsewhere Liepmann defines honor as "the totality [*Inbegriff*] of those qualities that are indispensable to a person for the fulfillment of their particular functions" or "that determine their specific worth" (Liepmann 1906, 227, 232).

24. I shall leave the term 'true personal quality' undefined, but I believe that its meaning will become sufficiently clear for the purposes of the arguments in which it appears.

25. Liepmann 1909, 14; cf. Liepmann 1906: 228, 246.

26. Varieties of this analysis are widespread, not only in Germany (Hirsch 1967, 1 gives extensive references), but also elsewhere. For instance, an Argentinian jurist who makes no reference to the German literature defines the prevailing judicial notion of honor as follows: *Es el sentimiento que cada uno tiene de su propria dignidad (aspecto subjectivo), honor propriamente dicho según unos, y la estimación que los demás tienen de nosotros (aspecto objectivo), u honra, que se trasunta en la reputación* (Rivanera 1961, 88, cf. 188 f; on this use of *honor* to mean internal honor and *honra* to mean external honor, see Beysterveldt 1966, 30–35). An Italian definition is very similar: *Inteso in senso soggettivo, esso [i.e., l'onore] si identifica con il sentimento che ciascuno ha della propria dignità morale [. . .] Inteso, invece, in senso oggettivo, è la stima o l'opinione che gli altri hanno di noi* (Musco 1974, 1, quoting an official source). Liotta (1980, 203), in describing the prevailing doctrine in Italian law, gives all three elements mentioned by Liepmann; *intimo valore morale della persona, conscienza della propria dignità*, and *stima dei terzi*.

he means 'my reputation as an honorable man'. This leaves open the question of why Phelps does not actually say 'my reputation' or 'my good name', but Liepmann could answer to this that the weighty word 'honor' is appropriate in these contexts because of the particular seriousness of the circumstances. And when Nathan Garrideb suggests that the American saw something as a reflection on his honor, Liepmann would say that the word 'honor' is being used here in its basic sense. Presumably, the word is also used in its basic sense in a phrase like 'a man of honor.' To interpret the phrase as meaning a man who is well thought of, or as meaning a man who has a strong sense of his own worth, would obviously be wrong; whereas to interpret it as meaning a man who possesses certain good qualities is quite plausible.

Liepmann can also add that the reason for the American's anger was (in Nathan's view) that what he thought Nathan had done had injured his sense of his own worth as an honest man. The injury, in other words, was to his subjectified honor. I take it that in Liepmann's view the word 'honor' is used to refer to subjectified honor in a phrase like 'it was an injury to his honor' when such a phrase is used in a context that excludes the possibility of interpreting 'honor' as referring to reputation.

At first blush it may seem that Liepmann's subjectified honor and objectified honor differ from each other only in respect of the person whose opinion is in question: there are my true qualities and corresponding worth (honor), there are what the world believes to be my qualities and corresponding worth (objectified honor), and there are what I believe to be my qualities and corresponding worth (subjectified honor). But this is not, and for good reason, what Liepmann in fact says. The idea behind objectified honor is in essence a simple one: the world believes that I possess certain important good qualities; it therefore holds me in a certain estimation; that estimation is of considerable value to me, and anything that tends to diminish it is therefore objectionable to me. The idea behind subjectified honor, however, is far more complicated. I myself (let us say) also believe that I possess certain important good qualities; I also hold myself in a certain estimation; and that estimation too is of considerable value to me, and anything that diminishes it is highly unwelcome to me. But the kind of thing that tends to diminish my objectified honor is different from the kind of thing that tends to diminish my estimation of myself. If I am, and have hitherto been known to be, an honest man, and you publish an article in the newspaper accusing me of a theft with which I know that I actually had no connection whatsoever, others may believe you, but I will not. Your article therefore tends to diminish my objectified honor, but not what I myself believe to be my worth. What it does tend to injure, in Liepmann's view, is my feeling (or sense) of honor, the feeling of my own worth that is engendered in me by my own honorable qualities and by their evaluation by others.[27] It is to this feeling that Liepmann applies the term "subjectified honor."

How are we to understand this concept? One might want to draw a distinction between what I consciously believe to be my worth and what I feel to be my worth. It would not be absurd for someone to say, "I know that I'm actually quite a decent person, but I *feel* as if I'm totally worthless."[28] Does this exemplify the feeling of self-worth that Liepmann has in mind? I think not. It seems reasonable to assert that if I am subjected to (let us say) verbal abuse day in, day out, then it will tend to lower my feeling of self-worth (using the term in the sense just indicated); and this may be a most serious injury.[29] But if—to take an example that Liepmann himself uses[30]—you accuse me of being a thief on a single occasion when there are no witnesses present, then my feeling of self-worth (in this sense) is not likely to be affected.

What Liepmann actually has in mind is therefore neither a mere belief nor a mere feeling. His "feeling of honor" seems rather to be a combination of the two. I hold certain more or less conscious beliefs about my own worth, and we will take it that these are generally of a favorable nature. Some of these beliefs are based on the self-ascription of qualities that have nothing to do with my honor: I think well of myself, for instance, because I am an excellent bridge player. Such a belief, though it may form part of my feeling of self-worth, does not form part of my feeling of honor.[31] In contrast, the beliefs that I am honest, that I am (if a man), brave, that I am (if a woman) chaste—these are

27. Liepmann 1909, 14: *das durch die eigenen Qualitäten und ihre Schätzung bei anderen in uns entstehende Gefühl des eigenen Wertes, das 'E h r g e f ü h l'.* Cf. Liepmann 1906, 228.
28. The converse is perhaps more difficult to imagine, but someone could surely say, "I know I've done some terrible things, yet in my heart of hearts I don't feel that I'm particularly bad," or "I know I'm a pretty worthless fellow, yet in my heart of hearts I feel that I'm just as good as the next man."
29. Liepmann 1906, 229.
30. Liepmann 1909, 16.
31. Liepmann 1906, 245–46.

indeed part of my feeling of honor, since it is the possession of such qualities that constitutes my honor.

Now assume that in my presence you ascribe to me dishonorable characteristics (e.g., in asserting that I am a thief) or that you simply express your disdain or contempt for me (e.g., by calling me a swine or by some nonverbal act).[32] I find this an unpleasant or painful experience. The mere fact that you have shown that your beliefs differ from mine is not enough to account for my distress: people are continually making it evident in various ways that their beliefs differ profoundly from my own, even on topics of great importance, without upsetting my equanimity. Obviously, my belief as to my own honorableness has a special emotional significance for me, and the combination of the belief and the complex of sentiments associated with it is, I think, what Liepmann meant by my feeling of honor.

Liepmann's account of insult, according to which it is an act that tends to injure a person's feeling of honor,[33] can, I believe, be shown to be unsatisfactory. Its most obvious weakness is that it blurs the distinction between *being* insulted and *feeling* insulted. To criticize Liepmann's theory of insult with the care that it deserves would, however, take up a disproportionate amount of space, and I shall therefore not embark on such a criticism here. At this point I merely wish to observe that Liepmann's model of honor is a complex one, made up of three elements that are very different from each other: personal qualities, reputation, and the feeling of honor (which, as we have seen, is itself a complicated and perhaps problematic concept). There is of course nothing inherently wrong with a complex model; but if a simple model can account equally well for the facts, then it is naturally to be preferred.

Liepmann's ideas are essentially a sophisticated version of what I take to be the most commonly held nonjuristic theory of honor, the one that views inner honor as a personal quality (honorableness),[34] and outer honor as reputation (for honorableness). The connection between inner and outer honor is thus established, though one can also have either one without the other. This view of honor (which I shall

32. Liepmann 1906, 247.
33. Liepmann 1906, 250: *Die Ehrenkränkung ist eine Handlung, welche geeignet ist, einen Menschen in seinem Ehrgefühl zu verletzen;* similarly, Liepmann 1906, 239, 246.
34. Cf. Barber 1957, 49.

refer to as the *bipartite theory*) appears in many descriptive studies,[35] and also in a recent philosophical work.[36] The authors of the descriptive studies also mention, of course, various other meanings and shades of meaning, but these need not concern us here; nor will we deal with variant versions of the bipartite theory.[37]

We know already how the bipartite theory explains what Phelps says; on this view he is talking about his reputation. The bipartite theory can also deal with the American (as viewed by Nathan). Its proponents can simply say that the American believes that his honorableness—that is, his honesty or something similar—is being doubted. A bipartite theorist might go on to argue that there is no need to postulate a special 'feeling of honor' in order to account for the American's anger. It could happen, for instance, that a man of intelligence is angered when he is treated as a fool, or that a prominent woman is angered if she is treated as if she were a nobody; yet we do not usually speak of a special 'feeling of intelligence' or 'feeling of prominence'. It seems rather that there is a whole variety of ways in which one can treat a person as having less worth than they really have, and that all varieties of such treatment are apt, in certain circumstances, to produce a negative reaction of some kind in the person who is treated in that way.

But the bipartite theory still faces various problems. The most obvious is that it does not account for insults. Calling me a swine cannot, as has been noted, affect my inner honor, my honorableness; and it may equally well not affect my outer honor, my reputation (especially, but not exclusively, if there are no witnesses). Yet to say this to me is—for a European—a perfect example of an offense against my honor.

Both Liepmann's theory and the bipartite theory also face the following problem. A man who has lost his honor is treated (let us say)

35. For instance, Morel 1964, 625–26; Jouanna 1968, 599, 607; and Barber 1985, 13–14. McKendrick (1984, 313) has much the same distinction in mind when she refers to "the honour = virtue versus honour = reputation debate."

36. Taylor 1985 (which, it should be said, is only peripherally concerned with honor). She writes of "a virtue or set of virtues which constitute a person's 'honor'" (1985, 110), but also of honor as being "public reputation" (1985, 54).

37. For instance, the one proposed by the philosopher James Collins (1968): "Honor may mean the public respect that is due to a person because he has certain qualities of character or has accomplished certain things. But, when we say that a person is a man of honor, we usually mean that he has a specific character trait which can be described best as *personal integrity.*"

with distrust or contempt. Assume that honorableness consists in the possession of some particular quality, for instance, courage. Then we might say, "It is because N has lost his reputation for courage that we treat him with contempt." But this is clearly wrong: it is not because (we believe that) N has lost his reputation for courage that we treat him thus, it is simply because (we believe that) he is a coward.

The alternative (according to the theories that interest us here) would be to say, "It is because N has lost his courage that we treat him with contempt." But this too is questionable: quite likely N was never courageous—it is just that we have only at this moment become aware of it. And even if we now realize that he was always a coward at heart, we cannot, I submit, retrospectively strip him of his honor. This is perhaps especially clear in the case of qualities such as fidelity to one's word or chastity. Henry's honor is intact until he breaks his promise, just as Jane's is until she finally succumbs to the importunities of her lover, and José's until his wife cuckolds him.[38]

In fact the possession of honor is not like the possession of a true personal quality. We may say, for instance, that Jane was clever before she fell on her head, and stupid afterwards, or that Samson lost his strength when his hair was cut. In cases of this kind we believe that some change of disposition has occurred in the individual. But a man may lose his honor without any such change: the fact that he has (say) tamely submitted to being insulted does not necessarily make him a different person. To have honor seems, then, to be like being American (in the sense of possessing U.S. citizenship) or being poor—a quality relating to the external circumstances of the individual, which, while it *may* change him when acquired or shed, does not *necessarily* do so. Like poverty, it may be closely related to certain true personal qualities without itself being one.

Honorableness—in the sense of being worthy of honor—*is* a true personal quality; what I have suggested is that you may have honor

38. The distinction that interests us here—between someone who is dishonorable by nature and someone who has lost his honor—is made clearly in Old Norse. A *níðingr* is "a person who has actually performed a shameful action" (Meulengracht Sørensen 1983, 31); "in general one becomes a *níðingr* only through an act that dishonors one" (Gehl 1937, 117). Gehl contrasts the term with words like *argr* and *mannfýla*, which refer to men who have the character traits (cowardice, an inclination to play the passive role in homosexual relations, lack of manliness) that are characteristic of dishonorable people. The contrast has analogues in modern English: I may be dishonest from birth, but I become a criminal only after I have committed a crime.

without being honorable, and that you may be honorable without having honor. Respectability stands in a fairly similar relationship to respect.

It would be possible to continue more or less indefinitely presenting theories of honor and showing the weak points of each one; but I think that this small sample will suffice. It may seem even that the search for a theory of honor is misguided—that the word covers a wide variety of concepts, none of which fit together in any clear way.[39] I shall now try to show that this is not so, or at any rate, not entirely so.

I suggest that we look on honor as a right, roughly speaking, the right to be treated as having a certain worth. I shall generally refer to it as a right to respect, but this is only a *pis aller.*[40] What honor is a right to is not the same in all cases, and I am unable to offer a precise general characterization. My main concern is to argue that honor is a right rather than that is it is a right to some particular thing.

The idea that honor is a right to respect fits insults well: to call you a swine is a clear infringement of such a right. It also fits both the examples from the Sherlock Holmes stories. Phelps is afraid that he will lose his right to the respect of others, and the American (as viewed by Nathan Garrideb) is angry because his right to the respect of others has been doubted.

The contrast between inner and outer honor reflects the two-sidedness of the relevant notion of a right, for honor (I suggest) is a *claim-right,* that is, "a right that something be done by another."[41] On the one side is the bearer, who has something about him that gives him a right to respect; and on the other is the world, which has a duty to treat the bearer with respect. In the story of the three Garridebs, our attention is concentrated on the bearer's right, while in the story of the naval treaty, it is concentrated on the world's duty. In the latter story

39. Cf. Billacois 1990, 33: "the French word *honneur,* which can be seen as a vague crossroads where women's honour, valour in battle, a good reputation in society and even honour in business meet"; and Gilbert 1976, 77: "Honour, by definition, is vague, imprecise and ever changing."

40. For the history of the theory that honor is a right to respect, see appendix 1 below. In what follows I shall take the notion of respect for granted, although in fact it demands extended analysis and is the subject of a considerable philosophical literature.

41. Sumner 1987, 48. Sumner contrasts the claim-right with the liberty-right, "a right to do something or not as one pleases." Other authors make the same distinction, but use different terminology (Sumner 1987, 48 n).

the question of whether Phelps really has that which entitles him to honor is not examined (though there is a tacit assumption that he does). What matters is whether the world will continue to believe that it has a duty to treat him with respect.

It may be appropriate, before going any further, to say a word about the concept of a *title to a right*. This notion is implied by certain phrases in the preceding paragraph ('something about him that gives him a right to respect,' 'that which entitles him to honor'), and it will appear more than once again in the course of this essay. I have taken this notion from the work of Alan White, who asserts that "to have a right is necessarily to have it in virtue of something, either of some feature of one's situation or of having been given it by someone who had the right, authority or power to give it [. . .] we must be careful not to confuse the ground in virtue of which we have a right with the right which we have in virtue of that ground."[42] He adds that

> There are many diverse things which in practice we commonly admit as possible or actual [. . .] grounds of rights of various kinds. Thus a ground of a right may be: (i) A rule, as when [. . .] the university regulations give a student the right to resit an examination. (ii) A principle, as when a murderer is denied any right of inheritance from his victim on the principle that no one should profit by his own wrong [. . .] (v) A contract, promise, or authorization, as when in return for payment I give someone the right to use my water supply [. . .] (x) The subject's position or role, as father, teacher, doctor, or husband or his identity as a human being, all of which give rise, arguably at least, to various rights connected with the qualities of such roles or such an identity.[43]

His conclusion is that "that in virtue of which one has a right, the ground of the right, is what entitles one. It is one's title."[44]

To return now to the main line of our argument, a look at another right may help to strengthen the point that the inner-outer contrast derives from the two-sided nature of claim-rights. Consider a university student who is in trouble—let us say that his grades have been very poor. It is possible that the university will decide to expel him, that is, his

42. White 1984, 93–94.
43. White 1984, 111.
44. White 1984, 114.

right to continue to study at the university is in danger. This right is like Phelps's honor: it is external to the student in the sense that whether it continues to exist depends for all practical purposes on how others judge his actions.

Now imagine another student, one who has good grades and who has been accepted at an excellent graduate school. I say to someone, "She shouldn't be there. She's just not smart enough. Sure she got good grades, but that was only because she worked day and night, had special tutoring, and cozied up to her professors. She'll be in the best department of theoretical physics in the country, but she hasn't got what it takes to do real research." The student could reasonably view this statement as casting doubt on her right to be in that department. And this doubt relates, as it were, to the internal aspect of her right, for I would be talking about true personal qualities of hers, namely, her intelligence and creativity. Yet these qualities are obviously quite distinct from her right to be in the department. In the same way, the personal qualities of the American that one might be tempted to identify with his honor (his integrity or his veracity or his moral character or whatever), though they may be part of what *entitles* him to honor, are not *identical* with his honor.

In what follows I shall sometimes use such phrases as 'inner honor', 'honor with an inner sense', 'the internal aspect of honor', and the like. In all such cases what I have in mind are instances in which the word 'honor'[45] is used in a way that directs our attention to the personal qualities that entitle someone to honor. In such cases one can, without doing violence to the context, substitute the name of some true personal quality for the word 'honor'. I shall use the phrase 'outer honor' in an analogous fashion.

In a given society, honor will be allocated according to certain rules. Now honor is not only something one can have, it is also something that one can lose. This is not a logically necessary concomitant of possessing a right to respect. A person may have an indefeasible right to respect as, say, a human being or as a parent. But I take losableness to be a defining feature of the kind of right to respect that interests us here: if one cannot lose it, then it is not *personal honor*, that is, honor in

45. Here, as in various other places, by 'honor' I mean not only the English word 'honor' but also the various words for honor in the other major modern European languages.

the sense that concerns us here.[46] There will therefore be, in addition to the rules about conferring honor, rules about losing honor. Such rules could in principle be of various kinds: it might be the case, for instance, that the king has the power at will to strip a person of their honor. But generally the rules in question relate to a *code of honor* (and I shall take the existence of such a code to be another defining feature of personal honor). These are rules that are incumbent on the person of honor as such; the price of breaking them is loss of honor. One might have a rule, for instance, that all and only the rich have honor, so that when a rich man is reduced to beggary he also loses his honor.[47] In the real world, however, the retention of honor seems to depend at least in part on following rules that are different in nature from "stay rich." The kind of rules I have in mind are "be generous and hospitable" or "keep your promises."[48]

There are also other groups of rules that deal with honor, for instance, rules about the duties that various kinds of people owe to the person of honor as such, and rules about settling disputes concerning honor (some of the latter, as we shall see in chapter 5, will in certain circumstances be part of the code of honor).

Let us now for a moment imagine somewhat different stories for the student in trouble and for Phelps. The student is expelled because of his poor grades, but did not deserve to be, since the poor grades were the result of a debilitating illness that has now passed, and the university regulations have special provisions for such cases. Holmes fails to recover the naval treaty, and Phelps is universally held responsible for its loss, but wrongly, for he was not even in the slightest degree negligent.

In such circumstances we may be tempted to say, "He *really* has a right to remain at the university (or to respect), but the university (or

46. Other types of honor are discussed in chapter 4.
47. Cf. Jones 1959, 61–64 on the importance of wealth in the medieval German notion of honor.
48. The notion of a rule is a capacious one, and philosophers have not so far made much progress either in distinguishing it from allied concepts or in sorting out the various types of rule that exist (cf. Gilbert 1992, 403). I shall take full—perhaps overfull—advantage of the capaciousness of the term, and will sometimes use the word to include what might more properly be referred to as values or standards or ideals of conduct. This is not because I consider the distinctions involved to be unimportant, but simply because I want to avoid dealing with them.

24

the world) has reached the wrong conclusion." There are in fact two different views of rights: the realistic one, which sees them as being assigned by people or institutions, as when we might say that, whatever the reason for the poor grades, the student does not have a right to stay at the university if the authorities decide to expel him; and the idealistic one, which sees rights as being assigned by the application of rules to facts, as when we might say that, whatever the authorities may decide, the student does have a right to stay on if his poor grades were caused by his illness, and the rules make provision for such cases.[49]

The sharpness of the contrast between inner and outer honor arises in part because they tend to ally themselves with different views of rights. When we ask, for instance, whether someone is a man of honor, that is, when our attention is concentrated on the bearer of the right, we are normally taking an idealistic view: we are asking whether he possesses the qualities that (should) endow him with honor, not whether the world recognizes him as possessing such qualities. When the American (as Nathan believes) sees Nathan's having written to Holmes as a reflection on his honor, what disturbs the American is probably not his belief that he is being presented to Holmes as a man whose honesty needs to be investigated; being an honest man, he knows that Holmes's investigation will vindicate his honor. It is rather his belief that in writing the letter Nathan is manifesting doubt as to his honesty. The American (we continue to view the situation as Nathan believes it to be) knows himself to be an honest man; and when he sees Nathan as casting a reflection on his honor, it is unlikely that he is thinking of his honor as something that the world accords to him. The chances are rather that he is viewing his honor as something to which his personal qualities entitle him, irrespective of what the world may believe. He is taking, that is, an idealistic view.

The opposite occurs when attention is concentrated on the world. For instance, when Phelps says to Holmes, "You have saved my honor," the natural way to understand this is not as meaning "By recovering the treaty you have placed me in a position where, according to the

---

49. Contrast, for instance, the notions of guilt and innocence: if, given the facts of the case and the law, a person is innocent of a crime, then we will continue to call that person innocent even if the highest courts have confirmed a verdict of guilty. The distinction between what I have called the 'idealistic' and the 'realistic' views of rights is my own, but I would be surprised if it (or something similar) has not already been made elsewhere in the literature.

rules of the code, my honor is saved" but rather "By recovering the treaty before the world learned that I had lost it, you have saved me from being regarded as dishonorable." Phelps is implicitly adopting the realistic view.

I wrote above that Phelps was afraid that he would lose his right to respect. Under an idealistic view of rights, this seems very doubtful. But Phelps, even if he is confident that his behavior has been beyond reproach, may say to himself, "Everyone will be convinced that I am not to be trusted, and nothing will ever change their minds. I shall no longer be in a position where I can insist on being treated as trustworthy. If I were to make demands of that kind, I would merely make myself laughable or pitiable." If these are his thoughts, then it seems reasonable to say that he fears that he will lose his right to be treated as trustworthy.

The contrast between the idealistic and the realistic view of rights also appears in the student cases. When I ask about the successful student, "Does she really have a right to be in that department?" the natural way to understand this is as a question about the student's abilities, and not about whether the authorities recognize her as having a right to be in the department. As for the student in danger of being expelled, imagine that I intervene in the matter and succeed in persuading the authorities not to expel him. The student might say to me, "If you hadn't stepped in, I'd have lost the right to continue my studies here." Here the speaker is clearly adopting the realistic view.

In sum, the internal quality of inner honor does not merely arise from the fact that we are looking at the bearer of the right, but also from the view of rights that we tend to adopt; and the external quality of outer honor arises in an analogous fashion.

It will be evident from the preceding discussion that the world plays two different roles in relationship to Phelps, just as the university plays two different roles in relation to the student with poor grades: it owes a duty, but it also has the power to determine that duty. The university, being a large organization, will naturally assign this power to some specific body within the university; and the world may do the same— it may establish a court of honor of one kind or another. The university's own judgment may even be overridden by that of a higher authority—a court of law may force it to reinstate a student who has been wrongfully expelled. This also has its analogy in the world of honor, as may be illustrated by a case that arose among the British garrison on Minorca in 1766. A certain Captain Robinson repeatedly insulted a fellow officer, Captain Beilby, saying to him, for instance, "Is that the way you march your guard, you shitten dirty fellow?" Despite this and similar remarks, Beilby failed to challenge Robinson to a duel. As a result other officers refused to associate with Beilby: this was the outcome of the world's verdict. Now at that time the Courts Martial functioned also as courts of honor; and so the unfortunate Beilby was court-martialed and convicted for "having repeatedly received from Captain Robinson [. . .] language unbecoming the character of an officer and a gentleman without taking proper notice of it [. . .]" The verdict was approved by the Lieutenant-Governor of Minorca, and it was only eventually overturned by the Judge Advocate General in England. He wrote, "I do not conceive that the sentence of a Court of Justice can at any rate be supported which awards a punishment for neglecting to seek a method of redress forbidden as well by the military as the common law."[50] What effect this verdict had on the world, that is, whether it induced the other officers to treat Captain Beilby more kindly, is not recorded; but at any rate Beilby was spared the punishment imposed by the Court Martial, suspension from pay and duty for one year.

The theory that honor is a right can be strengthened by a close examination of why the American got angry. Once again I want to view the situation not as it really is, where the American is dishonorable and Nathan does not doubt his honor; nor as Nathan believes it to be, where the American is honorable and Nathan does not doubt his honor; but rather as Nathan presumes that the American believes it to be, where the American is honorable and Nathan does doubt his honor. On this view Nathan Garrideb, in all likelihood, does not ask himself, "Is this fellow a man of honor?" but rather something like, "Is this fellow really telling the truth, or is he trying to trick me in some way?" And in writing to Holmes, Nathan no doubt also presents the question in approximately the latter form. Nathan is not primarily interested in the American's character, or his past, or his future: the main

---

50. Gilbert 1976, 77, 80–81.

thing that matters to him is whether, on just this particular occasion, the man is telling the truth.

Now when you in some way express doubt about my honesty, whether to me or to others, I may well feel angry, very likely specifically angry towards you. But I may also feel inhibited in my anger if I do not believe that I have good reason to be angry with you, and (roughly speaking) I have good reason only if you have done something wrong. The thing you have done wrong in this case will usually be that you have failed in the duty to treat me as an honest man. This duty is the correlate of my right to be treated as an honest man, and this in turn is a right that derives from (or is identical with) my honor.

Thus it is that when Nathan sees the American getting angry—and we may assume that the American showed himself specifically to be angry with Nathan—he makes sense of it by assuming that the American was viewing what he thought that he, Nathan, had done as a reflection on his honor. A reasonable man would of course not be angry with Nathan for wanting to check up on such a fantastic story when produced by a perfect stranger; but it is easy enough to imagine a somewhat unreasonable man being angry.[51]

Barber, in his study of the English drama, in essence adopts the bipartite theory. He distinguishes between 'honor' used in the sense of 'reputation' and 'honor' in the sense of 'honorableness'. Now he also notes a large group of occurrences that are "equivocal," that is, occurrences in which the word makes equally good sense in its context irrespective of which of these two interpretations is applied. One of the many instances given by Barber is the following passage from Shakespeare:

How with mine honor may I give him that,
Which I have given to you?[52]

---

51. A friend of mine who is in business once told me the following story. An accountant was supposed to check that my friend's warehouse contained the goods that my friend had declared it to contain; my friend has a strong interest in ensuring that the accountant's check should not be unduly thorough. When the accountant said he wanted to examine the contents of the boxes in a certain part of the warehouse, my friend pretended to become angry with him for doubting his word, and the accountant backed down. The accountant probably viewed my friend as honest but unreasonable; like Nathan Garrideb, he was wrong on both counts.

52. *Twelfth Night,* 3.4.216–17.

Barber offers two glosses: "This behaviour is not consistent with my maintaining my integrity of character," and "If I behave like this I shall lose my reputation."[53]

The same "equivocation" has been noted with regard to the various Old Norse words meaning 'honor': "It is characteristic here precisely that the distinction between a subjective and an objective point of view (the sense of honor as a character trait and the judgment of others), which seems so obvious, cannot always be made."[54]

The frequent need to resort to "equivocation" in glossing the word 'honor' is a major weakness of the bipartite theory. Consider, by way of comparison, a word like the Arabic *ghanam*. We hear people using the word to refer to a group of goats, we hear them using the word to refer to a group of sheep, and we hear them using it to refer to a group that contains both sheep and goats. A bipartite theory might say that in the last case the sentence 'here are some *ghanam*' either means 'here are some sheep', or 'here are some goats', or both these things at once. But this is surely more complicated than necessary: unless we had good reason to do otherwise, we would simply say that the term covers both sheep and goats, in other words, that it means something like 'small stock' or 'capridae'. (And this is in fact the case.)

In the same way, interpreting honor as a right provides a far more natural account of a large number of occurrences than does the bipartite theory. This interpretation will cover not only many occurrences where 'honor' is used in an external way, and many occurrences where it is used in an internal way, but also many occurrences that the bipartite theory would view as equivocal. I would propose to gloss the lines from Shakespeare as 'If I behave like this, I shall lose my right to respect', the assumption being that the speaker himself, like every decent person, subscribes to the code under which his worth would be diminished. If this interpretation is correct, then there is no equivocation; and I assume that many at least of the Old Norse examples can be dealt with in a similar fashion.

53. Barber 1957, 54.
54. Gehl 1937, 80.

3

THE SENSE OF HONOR

THE VARIETY OF MEANINGS OF THE WORD 'HONOR'

The noun 'honor', like its equivalents in the other major modern European languages, is used in a wide variety of ways and I do not want to suggest that the analysis offered in the preceding chapter applies to all of them. For instance, 'honor' may mean 'distinction' ("He that had the honor of taking the French king prisoner"),[1] or 'mark of distinction or esteem' ('It is a great honor to be elected a Fellow of the Royal Society'), or 'esteem' ("to hold a statesman in high honor").[2]

Syntactic criteria can to some extent help in isolating the occurrences that interest us: when 'honor' refers to a right it is always possible to precede the word with a possessive pronoun ('her honor') or with a noun in the possessive ('Jane's honor'). But the converse (that whenever the word 'honor' appears in such a syntactic context, then it refers to a right) is not true. We say things like 'they named the college in his honor', and we use "the respectful form of address or of reference, 'your honour', 'his honour', 'their honours'."[3] Other exceptions appear in older layers of the language: the first edition of the *Oxford English Dictionary* (s.v. "honour," sb. section 1), for instance, quotes the following from the year 1703: "To shew my honour for them." Here 'honor' means something like 'esteem' or 'respect'.

If 'honor' is legitimately used in many different senses, why should we here confine ourselves largely to the instances where 'honor' can be interpreted as referring to a right? In essence it is because these are the distinctive uses of 'honor'. In its other uses it is generally easy enough to replace the word in a fairly satisfactory fashion by some other word or short phrase, whereas in those that interest us it is difficult to find

---

1. Barber 1957, 71. Occurrences of the word in similar phrases, e.g., "the second artist . . . to be accorded the honor of designing the annual Christmas seal," are interpreted by *Webster's Third New International Dictionary*, s.v. "honor," as meaning "a special prerogative."

2. This last example is taken from *Webster's Third New International Dictionary*, s.v. "honor."

3. Barber 1957, 77.

such a replacement. These are therefore the occurrences that have puzzled people. When they have asked what honor is, they have not usually been troubled by sentences like "this year the honour of a steward's green rosette was conferred upon me";[4] but they have wondered what the word stands for in sentences like 'for John it was a matter of honor to enroll in the Guards'.

Now the main purpose of this essay is to contribute to the development of a concept of honor that can be used cross-culturally. As it is used in the major modern European languages, the word 'honor' obviously has far too wide a range of meanings for this purpose. In many of its uses we can, I have suggested, replace it with other, less protean words. But if there is indeed a distinctive group of uses of the word, and if that distinctive group relates to a concept that is useful in describing non-European cultures, then for such purposes we may reasonably preserve the word 'honor', using it now in a limited and technical way to refer only to the concept in question.

The great variety of meanings of the word 'honor' is no more than a reflection of its long and complex history. And that history is not just one of peaceful linguistic drift. For centuries it was widely agreed that honor was something both important and desirable, and attempts were continually being made to capture the word for a particular set of values. In the seventeenth century honor was probably more important in England than ever before or after, and yet different people had very different, and often quite contradictory, ideas as to the kind of behavior demanded by honor.[5] In the mid-eighteenth century the eponymous villain of Fielding's *Jonathan Wild* (first published in 1743) gives a speech on the subject of honor, where he says, among other things,

> But alas! Gentlemen, What Pity is it, that a Word of such sovereign Use and Virtue should have so uncertain and various an Application, that scarce two People mean the same Thing by it. Do not some by Honour mean Good-nature and Humanity, which weak Minds call Virtues? How then! Must we deny it to the Great, the Brave, the Noble, to the Sackers of Towns, the Plunderers of Provinces, and the

---

4. E. Œ. Somerville and Martin Ross, *Occasional Licenses*. The story is included in *Some Experiences of an Irish R.M.*, which appeared in 1899; the story must have been published separately not long before.

5. Barber 1957, 145.

Conquerors of Kingdoms? Were not these Men of Honour? And yet
they scorned those pitiful Qualities I have mentioned.[6]

Wild goes on to argue, item by item, that honor does not include the
idea of honesty, that it is not truth, and that it does not "consist of what
the Vulgar call Cardinal Virtues." His conclusion is that "a Man of
Honour is he that is called a Man of Honour; and while he is so called,
he so remains, and no longer." These remarks are designed to show the
depth of Wild's cynicism; but the analysis that lies behind them is a
serious one, and in it Fielding puts his finger on two of the central peculiarities of honor: the one that interests us here, which is that different people held very different, even contradictory, ideas about the
qualities that entitle a man to honor (it is likely indeed that even the
same individual sometimes had inconsistent ideas on this subject);
and the one that interested us in the preceding chapter, the contrast
between inner and outer honor. Wild's solution to the problem this
presents is to equate the man of honor with the man who is treated by
the world as having his honor intact, while Fielding himself, by putting
this line of argument in the villain's mouth, implicitly adopts the opposite position, that the man of honor is a virtuous man, and that
honor does indeed consist of virtues such as good-nature,[7] humanity,
and honesty.

Many definitions of honor are not dispassionate analyses but rather
intellectual moves in conflicts of one kind of another. Fielding, for instance, is attacking certain tendencies of his age. Just as Fielding attempts to identify honor with his values, so too there have been a
number of determined attempts to Christianize honor: to choose one
example among many, a German Protestant at the end of the nineteenth century defined the notion in a way that enabled him to write
that "no-one can value this honor more highly than a Christian."[8] In
France, in the eighteenth century, "the *philosophes* succeeded in changing the sense of the word 'honor' and in substituting their views for

6. Fielding 1932, 56. The passage comes from the beginning of book 1, chapter 13; it
is unchanged in the revised version of 1754. Similar thoughts are expressed in *Tom Jones*,
book 3, chapter 3 (Fielding 1974, 126–28).

7. On what Fielding meant by this, see Fielding 1974, 39 n.

8. Herrmann 1898, 227. A number of twentieth-century studies on honor and
Christianity are listed in the bibliography given in Thielicke 1982.

those of the old aristocracy."[9] Even after World War I, when the significance of honor among speakers of European languages was much diminished, both the Nazis and (to a much lesser extent) the Communists still tried to adapt the notion to their own ideologies.[10] The varied and tendentious definitions given by such analysts are a further source of the confusion that surrounds the word. For the differences of opinion about what honor is do not merely relate to what entitles one to honor, as, for instance, if one person maintains that high rank brings honor, and the other denies it, while still admitting that the nature of honor is such that in principle high rank *could* bring honor. Rather, these ideologically conditioned differences can relate to the question of what kind of thing honor is. In the individualistic Germany of the late nineteenth century, for instance, honor was again and again defined as a personal quality, much like integrity, and one that might well bring a man of honor into conflict with the society around him (Fielding would no doubt have approved); to the Nazis, however, with their collectivist outlook, such ideas were anathema, and for them honor tended to be a thing bestowed on the individual by the community (and this is also Jonathan Wild's view).

I have suggested two factors that help explain the remarkable amount of disagreement as to how the notion of honor should be analyzed: one is that the word 'honor' has a very wide range of meaning, the other that many different ideologies have tried to make the word their own. The pages that follow will suggest a third factor. Even if we analyze honor as a right, it turns out to be intimately connected with many things that are not rights, and it is easy to see why it is sometimes identified with these things. Pitt-Rivers is, I believe, wrong in claiming that honor, in one of its facets, is a sentiment; but it is certainly closely linked with a sentiment, just as it is closely linked with moral worth, reputation, self-respect, and most of the other things that theorists have proposed identifying it with.

9. Pappas 1982, 39.
10. For the Communists, see Tackmann 1975; for the Nazis, see Brezina 1987. The question of *why* honor has lost its importance in recent times remains unanswered. Such studies as I have seen on this subject—notably Berger 1970 (reprinted with insignificant alterations in Berger, Berger, and Kellner 1973, 83–96) and Angehrn 1982—are not much help.

THE HISTORY OF THE WORD 'HONOR'

It will be helpful, I think, to glance briefly at part of the history of the word 'honor' in Western Europe,[11] beginning with the Middle Ages. The easiest language to start with is German, since the notion of honor (*êre*) as it appears in the German literature of the high Middle Ages has been the subject of a fair amount of scholarly discussion.[12] It is generally agreed that word usually referred then to something like reputation, prestige, renown, standing, or worth in the eyes of others; though to this it must be added that *êre* was used in many different contexts, and already showed much of the slipperiness of its modern successors. For instance, in addition to those who gain, preserve, or lose honor, there are those who show honor to another (*êre bieten*) by treating the other as having worth; one can do a great variety of things *nâch êren*, in an honorable way, and in particular one can live in an honorable way; and it is said of a wedding feast that at it there was joy and *êre*.[13]

One issue the Germanists have discussed is whether *êre* was external or internal. The prevailing view derives from the work of Friedrich Maurer, who followed the bipartite theory of honor. He believed that the word began with an exclusively external sense (reputation, prestige, and the like), and that it was making a transition, still incomplete in our own time, to an exclusively internal sense (a virtue). He emphasized that, at least up to the early thirteenth century, the word *êre* is rarely used in a way that suggests that it might be referring to a character trait.[14] If, however, the views put forward in this book are correct, then the direction of development was not exactly what Maurer thought it was; and since his attention was slightly misdirected, a somewhat different view of the material is possible.

Êre was often doubly external, for among the qualities that endowed a man with *êre* in the sense of reputation or standing, some that are not true personal qualities were prominent; for instance, wealth, rank and

11. I use this term in a restricted sense, excluding Iceland, Ireland, and Scandinavia.
12. Martin 1984 gives references to the literature, to which may be added Fischer 1983.
13. These examples all come from Hartmann von Aue's *Iwein;* the last is from line 2442; Maurer 1951, 266 gives the references to the others.
14. Maurer 1970, which uses the detailed evidence mustered in Maurer 1951, 273–79.

power. Victory in battle was essential for the maintenance of honor;[15] and a literary historian who has examined the German Arthurian romances of the high Middle Ages remarks that the leading source of disgrace in every poem analyzed in her book is (to survive) defeat in battle.[16] It was only with the Renaissance that the idea appeared that one who fought valiantly (but survived) might preserve his honor even in defeat.[17] And where true personal qualities do appear in medieval German literature as bringing *êre* to a man, they are sometimes physical ones such as strength and beauty,[18] and sometimes psychological ones that we would probably not consider moral, notably high spirits (*hôher muot*) and lack of indolence (*ungemach*).[19]

Nevertheless, there is also evidence of moral virtues being a source of *êre:* fidelity (*triuwe*), courage, mercy to the vanquished, generosity, moderation, courtesy, and so on.[20] It is in this area that the future of the word lay, and the Germanists are agreed that the importance of moral qualities for *êre* is greater in the high Middle Ages than it was in earlier times, though still less than it was to be in later times.

It has never (to my knowledge) been suggested that *êre* might refer to a right, but there is good reason to believe that this sense also existed, at least by the end of the fourteenth century.[21] The word may already sometimes have had this meaning much earlier. Here, for instance, is a passage from Hartmann von Aue's *Iwein*, an Arthurian epic that was composed in about 1200. Six of the knights were talking to each other one evening, five of them seated, and the sixth, the unmannerly Sir Kay, lying down. Sir Kalogrenant, one of the seated knights, began to tell them a story. Now the queen (we know her to be Guinevere, though

15. As indicated by an early twelfth-century poet quoted by Zunkel (1975, 9): *Unde wirt er danne sigelôs, sô ist er immer êrenlôs* ('If he is then defeated, he will be evermore without honor').

16. Martin 1984, 199; see also Jones 1959, 20, 67–69, and for the French literature, Robreau 1981, 129, 150–52.

17. Zunkel 1975, 9, who quotes the famous words that Francis I is said to have written after the battle of Pavia (1525): *Tout est perdu fors l'honneur.* The king's actual words were rather different (Halkin 1949).

18. Martin 1984, 18, 47, 61.

19. Jones 1959, 72–73; Martin 1984, 171.

20. Martin 1984, 7, 17, 94, 127–28, 142; Jones 1959.

21. See the discussion of the guarantee in chapter 8, which deals with the notion as it appears in one part of late medieval law.

she is not named in the poem), on hearing them talking, rose from her bed, and

> crept so silently to the knights that none of them was aware of it until she had come very close to them and had fallen right into their midst. Kalogrenant alone jumped to his feet before her and welcomed her with a bow. Then Kay reacted in his usual manner: he hated to see anyone do anything worthy of praise, and he chastised him and questioned his honor because of it.[22] "Sir Kalogrenant," he said, "[. . .] None of us is so thoughtless that had he seen the queen he would not have proven himself as much of a gentleman as you did. Since none of us saw her, or for whatever reason we forgot ourselves and remained seated, you could have remained seated as well."[23]

The word *êre* occurs twice in the passage, being translated the first time as "anything worthy of praise" and the second time as "honor." In its second occurrence the word is part of the idiom *an eines êre sprechen* 'to speak against someone's honor'. Kay is saying that Kalogrenant's act, which seemed to be a courteous one, was not in fact so, apparently because it put the other knights to shame.

In principle, one could understand *êre* here as inner honor in the sense that the term has in the bipartite theory; that is, as a virtue, the relevant aspect of which in this context would be courtliness or good manners. The sentence that precedes Kay's speech could be translated, "Then Kay reacted in his usual manner: he hated anyone's honorableness, and for this reason he chastised Kalogrenant and questioned his honorableness." But few, if any, scholars would accept such an interpretation. *Êre* is so very often something external, something that one gains and loses, something that is shown to one by others, that only if no other interpretation is possible should it be taken to refer to a character trait.[24]

Maurer classifies both occurrences of *êre* in this passage under the general heading of 'reputation, standing, recognition'.[25] An external

22. *Do erzeicte aber Keiî / sîn alte gewonheit: / im was des mannes êre leit, / und beruoft in drumbe sêre / und sprach im an sîn êre* (Hartmann 1984, lines 110–13).

23. Hartmann 1984, 7–8.

24. "Honor is definitely a possession, not a quality" (Martin 1984, 17, referring to the use of *êre* in *Erec*, another of Hartmann's Arthurian romances).

25. *Ansehen* or *Anerkennung* (Maurer 1951, 276). Maurer also classes the other two occurrences of the idiom *an eines êre sprechen* in the poem under this heading.

way of understanding 'he spoke against his honor' here would be as meaning that Kay said something that harmed Kalogrenant's honor. The problem with this is that it does not quite fit the context. In the Arthurian tales Kay epitomizes the knight who fails to live up to the proper standards. Kalogrenant's prestige is not likely to be damaged by anything that Kay says, and indeed Kay, when he has finished his speech, is put firmly in his place by the queen, who says, "Those who understand you know your insults to be praise."[26]

It is not surprising, then, that Patrick McConeghy, whose translation of the passage is quoted above, takes the phrase to mean here that Kay *questioned* Kalogrenant's honor; in other words, that he expressed doubt about it, perhaps that he *tried* to harm it, but not that he actually succeeded in harming it. If we continue to understand *êre* in the kind of eternal sense that Maurer proposes, then we must view Kay as attacking Kalogrenant's standing, that is, not as lowering his standing, but as *attempting* to lower it. Kalogrenant had, by his gesture, gained in prestige, and Kay was trying to cut him down to size again. Under this interpretation, which seems to me a plausible one, the text would mean that Kay hated to see someone enjoying prestige, and so he attacked Kalogrenant's standing.

Now the way in which Kay tried to lower Kalogrenant's standing was by arguing that Kalogrenant had no right to it.[27] In this passage, then, the word *êre* in the phrase 'he spoke against his *êre*' could mean 'standing', but could also mean 'right to his standing.' I am not able to say which is the more plausible interpretation; but the two are certainly different from each other. When I assert, for instance, that McTaggart attacked my reputation, I mean that he tried to show that I do not have a right to my reputation; but it does not follow from this that the word 'reputation' refers to some kind of right. At any rate, even if *êre* does only mean 'standing' here, we can see from this passage that the transition to the meaning 'a right to a certain standing' is not going to be a difficult one.

A generation after Hartmann, the greatest of the medieval German

---

26. *Dîn schelten ist ein prîsen / wider alle die wîsen* (Hartmann 1984, lines 151–52).

27. One can of course attempt to lower a man's standing by saying something where what one says is *not* an argument against his right to that standing. The story goes, for instance, that at the height of the Cold War an American journalist who wanted to harm the career of a Soviet diplomatist succeeded in doing so by describing the unfortunate Russian in print as "friendly," "co-operative," and the like.

law books, the *Sachsenspiegel*, was written, and from that time on the law offers a mass of information about honor; in fact, Germany seems to be distinguished from other parts of Western Europe in the Middle Ages by the amount of attention that its law pays to the subject.[28] It is in the *Sachsenspiegel* that we first encounter the phrase *ehrlos und rechtlos* 'honorless and rightless'.[29] The exact meanings of these two terms, which are sometimes found together in the sources and sometimes separately, and of a related, but less common, term, *echtlos*, were debated at length in the nineteenth century; and though the problems involved are far from having been finally solved, a certain measure of agreement was reached in the early part of the twentieth century, since when the whole issue has been neglected. In the last extended study of the subject, Hubert Naendrup concluded that the three terms (and indeed various others as well) were often used interchangeably;[30] and it seems to be accepted by most authorities that this is true at least of 'honorless', 'rightless', and 'honorless and rightless'.[31] Such terms were applied to three main groups of people: those guilty of certain disgraceful misdeeds (e.g., theft, breach of faith); bastards; and followers of a variety of professions or ways of life that were looked down upon, for instance, actors and professional fighters. These people (with some distinctions between them) lacked certain rights that others enjoyed: judicial rights (e.g., to pass judgment, to testify), the right to be a guardian or ward, the right of inheritance, and the right to enfeoff or be enfeoffed; nor did wergild have to be paid for them.[32]

I do not want to assert that the evidence proves that in the German legal sources of the thirteenth century *êre* was a right. For one thing, it is not certain that *recht* meant 'a right'. Naendrup thought that it did,[33] but others believed, for instance, that it meant the legal status that one

28. Hübner 1930, 116.

29. *Deutsches Rechtswörterbuch*, s.v. ehr(en)los.

30. Naendrup 1905, 376.

31. Hübner 1930, 117.

32. Heusler 1885–86, 1:194; His 1920–35, 1:580.

33. Naendrup 1905, 303: *Die Bedeutung von 'recht', die [. . .] hier keine andere ist, als diejenige unseres heutigen Wortes Recht im subjektiven Sinne.* The history of the notion of a right remains largely unwritten, but it seems that (at least in Europe) the idea first takes clear shape in the later part of the Middle Ages. According to Villey 1964, it was William of Occam, in a work written in about 1332, who first produced a definition of the notion. See also Hart 1982, 165.

possessed as a result of one's rank,[34] or that it referred to a complex of purely judicial rights (*Gerichtsfähigkeiten*), such as the right to be a judge, a lay assessor (*Schöffe*), a witness, and the like.[35] For another, the fact—if it is a fact—that 'rightless' and 'honorless' could often be used interchangeably does not entail that they meant the same thing. But one can at least say that in the thirteenth century 'honor' often stands in a very close relationship with a word that, even if it does not exactly mean 'a right', at least refers to certain particular rights or to something like a right; and as I have mentioned, by the late fourteenth century there is, in my view, evidence that leaves no doubt that honor is being treated as a right.

The medieval use of the word 'honor' has not been studied so extensively in the other major languages of Western Europe as it has in German; for English and Italian, in fact, I have come across no studies at all, and for the languages of the Iberian Peninsula and of France there are not many.[36] But it is probably safe to assume that the medieval history of the idea of honor is roughly the same throughout Western Europe, and also that the changes in meaning that take place after the Renaissance are common to the region as a whole, though the time at which they occurred may have been very different from place to place.

For these changes, the best evidence, thanks to the work of C. L. Barber, is from England. The finding that interests us here is that "the use of the word *honour* in the sense 'honourableness of character' [. . .] is a relatively rare usage even in Shakespeare's day. This usage becomes more and more frequent in plays during the first half of the seventeenth century, and in the Restoration drama it is the commonest meaning of the word."[37] Now when Barber says that this is the commonest meaning of the word he does not mean that in every relevant

34. *Die altdeutsche Rechtssprache begnügte sich mit dem Worte Recht, um die Stellung auszudrücken, die man vermöge seines Standes in Ausübung jener persönlichen Rechte gegenüber den andern Menschen einnimmt* (Heusler 1885–86, 1:190).

35. Gierke 1895–1917, 1:417; His 1920–35; 1:579.

36. The main ones of which I am aware are Serrano Martínez 1956 and Robreau 1981. Smaller studies not mentioned by either of these authors include Settegast 1885; Settegast 1887; and Kettner 1890.

37. Barber 1985, 32; cf. Barber 1957, 96–97. Barber's account of *why* this change occurred (1985, 32–33; 1957, 99–100), though interesting, is far from exhaustive.

occurrence one can properly substitute the phrase 'honorableness of character' for 'honor':[38] this will clearly not work for phrases such as 'sense of honor' or 'laws of honor', which occur in the material that he classifies under the heading 'honorableness'.[39] He means rather that the noun 'honor' comes in Restoration drama to be used most commonly in contexts where attention is not mainly directed at how others value a person, but rather at certain personal qualities or a certain kind of behavior. An example of this usage is "They are women of honour, and will keep their words."[40]

The pace at which the internal aspect of honor came to be emphasized no doubt varied considerably from one Western European country to another. When the process started in English is unclear; all we know for certain is that it was already under way in the sixteenth century.[41] Maurer, whose general tendency is to emphasize the externality of the concept of *êre*, nevertheless sees internal content creeping into the word as early as the beginning of the thirteenth century;[42] but Jones says that "the sense of personal integrity or inner voice, did not become widespread before the middle of the eighteenth century."[43] Robreau believes that she can find occasional occurrences of the Old French *honor* in the sense of "qualities that lead one to show civility and courtesy to others" in the Arthurian prose romances of the late twelfth and the thirteenth century.[44] There is a famous passage by Rabelais that perhaps shows the word being used in an inner sense in the mid–sixteenth century: "Free people, well-born, well-instructed, conversing in good company, have by nature an instinct and a spur that always impels them to virtuous behavior and restrains them from vice: they call it *honor*" (*Gens liberes, bien nayz, bien instruictz, conversans en compaignies honnestes, ont par nature ung instinct et aguillon qui tousjours les poulse à faictz vertueux, et retire de vice: lequel ilz nommoyent honneur).*[45] The history of the word *onore,* which might be especially informative given the leading role that Italy played in these matters

38. See especially Barber 1957, 49.
39. Barber 1957, 243–44.
40. Barber 1957, 258; from the year 1681.
41. Cf. Kelso 1929, 96–106.
42. See especially Maurer 1951, 279.
43. Jones 1959, 6.
44. Robreau 1981, 25.
45. *Gargantua and Pantagruel,* book 1, chapter 57. I have taken the quotation from Burckhardt 1989, 426–27 (near the beginning of chapter 6).

during the Renaissance, remains (to the best of my knowledge) unexplored. A great Spanish scholar has written that "in contrast to the doctrine that honor depends in essence on the opinion of others, that honor is the same as reputation, [. . .] there exists in the Middle Ages as in the seventeenth century an individualistic view that places honor exclusively in honorable behavior, without regard to reputation."[46] It is not clear to me whether the individualistic view to which Menéndez Pidal refers is to be identified with one that emphasizes the internal aspect of honor; in any event, I am not aware of any passages from medieval Spanish literature in which the word *onra* (or the word *honor*) is used with emphasis on its internal aspect. The earliest such example noted by Serrano Martínez—and it remains for a long time an isolated one—is from the beginning of Act 2 of *La Celestina* by Fernando de Rojas (1499); and the sense of the passage in which it occurs is not clear to me.

At all events, by the nineteenth century the internal aspect of honor was prominent among speakers of all the major European languages. The change is probably just one small aspect of a great shift in sensibility that took place after the Renaissance. Maurer, in his various publications, has emphasized that the development in meaning that *Ehre* 'honor' undergoes as it moves from a medieval and external sense to a modern and internal one is paralleled by similar developments in the meaning of other words, for instance *Tugend* 'virtue' and *Leid* 'injury, sorrow'. And the changing usage that Barber points to is consistent with a broader difference that is said to have existed between sixteenth- and seventeenth-century England: an historian remarks on "the sixteenth-century lack of interest in men's private feelings," and writes that "it has been argued that Tudor men and women talked and wrote as though they had virtually no 'inner life' [. . .] The anatomising of private emotion came in only with Donne and the Jacobeans."[47]

I noted above that medieval German *êre* was generally external in two ways: in the sense that a man's *êre* lay in how others valued him along certain dimensions, and in the sense that some of the dimensions in question were not true personal qualities. The process that people have in mind when they refer to the transition from external to internal

---

46. Menéndez Pidal 1964, 159. Unfortunately, he gives no references.
47. Morris 1966, 18–19. Unfortunately, Morris does not give his source.

honor involves changes in both these things: honor (in their view) comes to be *naturally internal* in that the word refers to a person's qualities rather than what others think of those qualities; and it becomes *morally internal* in that the qualities on which honor is based come more and more to be moral virtues. It is important to observe that these (alleged) changes are logically independent of each other. The word 'honor' might have remained naturally external in that it meant something like reputation, while becoming morally internal in that the reputation in question came to be one for certain moral virtues. Equally, the word might have become naturally internal in that it came to refer to personal qualities, while remaining morally external in that these qualities were mainly or exclusively things like rank, wealth, physical strength, and beauty.

Barber is exceptional in that he is sensitive to the distinction between natural and moral internality (even though he does not note it explicitly). In analyzing his material, he groups it under various headings. Two of the main ones are R (mnemonic for Reputation) and H (mnemonic for Honorableness).[48] When he refers, in the passage quoted above, to the enormous increase of the use of 'honor' in the sense of 'honorableness of character', he is referring to an increase in the proportion of uses he classifies as H. The phrase 'honorableness of character' might lead one to assume that this category includes only material that is in his view both naturally internal and morally internal. In fact, however, it is designed to include only material that is naturally internal, and as a result includes some that is at the same time morally external. For example, "in Restoration comedy, a man of honour had to be a good wencher,"[49] and there are a number of occurrences of 'honor' in which the context indicates that the word refers to sexual virility. This is the case, for instance, of an occurrence in Dryden's comedy *Marriage à la Mode* (1671), where one character says, "You shall find that I am a man of honour."[50] Barber classifies this (and some other references to virility) under H, as indeed he should, given his conceptual framework; but virility is scarcely a moral virtue, so we would not be inclined to call this usage morally internal.

48. For the sake of simplicity I am ignoring his RH material, that is, the occurrences that he views as "equivocal." Its existence, like that of the various other of his categories that I ignore here, is essentially irrelevant to the argument of this section.

49. Barber 1957, 142.

50. Barber 1957, 250.

The increase in H that Barber detects is thus an increase in what he takes to be naturally internal use of 'honor'. Was there also an increase in occurrences of the word 'honor' where the speaker has in mind mainly moral virtues as the source of honor? This is not an inference that Barber himself draws from the statistical analysis of his data, though it would be possible, given the admirably explicit way in which they are presented, to reclassify them in such a way as to give a quantitative measure of the frequency of this usage in seventeenth-century drama. And even without such a reanalysis, one can unhesitatingly answer yes to the question. For though Barber's H material includes instances of (what he takes to be) naturally internal honor that are at least arguably not morally internal, the (alleged) naturally internal uses of the word are *usually* morally internal ones, so that broadly speaking the increasing proportion of H indicates an increase in uses of 'honor' where the speaker has in mind mainly moral virtues as the source of honor. Furthermore, Barber's material includes a great many instances that he classifies as R where there is reference to moral virtues; and there are strong indications that such references constitute an increasing portion of the R material as time goes on.

In this section I have operated with the bipartite theory of honor. I have noted that what Maurer and many others look on as a single process ('internalization') actually consists, under the bipartite theory, of two quite distinct changes: natural internalization and moral internalization. That the two are indeed wholly different from each other appears with particular clarity from Barber's material. What Barber takes to be the naturally internal uses of the word 'honor' are grouped under his H material; and while much of the H material is also morally internal, some is not. What Barber takes to be the naturally external uses of 'honor' are grouped under his R material; and while some of the R material is not morally internal, a large part of it is.

I now want to revert to the theory of honor that is central to this essay, the theory that the word is often used to refer to a right. The existence of a process of moral internalization does not present any challenge to that theory, for there is no difficulty about a right being based on the possession of certain virtues. Natural internalization is another matter. In chapter 2, I argued that occurrences of 'honor' in (fairly) modern usage that under a bipartite theory would be classified as naturally internal are in fact nothing of the sort. They do (in my view) have a kind of internality, but it is a nonnatural kind, for in such occurrences the word 'honor' does not refer to a personal quality but to a right. What gives the word an internal quality in such contexts is (I suggested) the fact that it is used in a way that directs our attention to the personal qualities that entitle a person to that right.

I do not, however, want to assert that 'honor' is *never* used in a naturally internal way. Already in the Middle Ages, words meaning 'honor' sometimes refer to things from which honor derives. One clear example is the use of *êre* to mean 'victory'.[51] As has been indicated, *êre* is rarely if ever used in a way that suggests that it may be referring to a virtue, and this is no doubt true of the medieval words for 'honor' in the other major Western European languages.[52] But as honor comes increasingly to be based on the possession of certain moral virtues, the same tendency shows itself, that is, the tendency to use the word 'honor' in a way that can be understood as referring to the things from which honor derives. The earliest example of such a usage in the *Oxford English Dictionary* (s.v. "honour," sb. section 2) is dated 1548: "The king of England has so great trust [. . .] in the honor and promise of the French kyng." In the English drama of the sixteenth, and above all of the seventeenth, century there are many occurrences that, like the one just quoted, invite a naturally internal interpretation. Thus one of Dryden's characters says, "My honour bids me succour the oppressed,"[53] and the same sense appears without personification in many other phrases from the seventeenth-century English drama, notably "I trust your honour" and such related expressions as "confidence in your honour," "suspect my honour," "distrust his honour."[54]

Now if we were to translate "My honour bids me succour the oppressed" into plain modern English, I believe we would render it as something like "my sense of honor impels me to help the oppressed." In the same way we might say "Jane's sense of honor prevented her from cheating." The phrase 'sense of honor' begins to appear in Bar-

---

51. Jones 1959, 67; Maurer 1970, 247. According to Serrano Martínez (1956, 37) the use of 'honor' in various European languages to refer to a fief and the like is another example; cf. Robreau 1981, 7–21 and Serra Ruiz 1969, 155.

52. Cf. Robreau 1981, 26–30.

53. This comes from *The Conquest of Granada,* 2d part (1671); I have quoted it from Barber 1957, 253.

54. Barber 1957, 246, 249, 251, 253, 254.

ber's material in the 1660s,[55] and I have not noted him as citing any similar phrase (e.g., 'sentiment of honor') from an earlier date. I assume—though without evidence—that once the phrase came into use it tended to supplant the use of 'honor' exemplified in the preceding paragraph; but even if this assumption is correct, the usage in question—which is, of course, a naturally internal one—may have persisted into modern times. I have not come across any unequivocal examples, but the following may be mentioned. In a Sherlock Holmes story a lady says to the great detective, "Here is the packet which will save Alexis. I confide it to your honour and to your love of justice. Take it! You will deliver it at the Russian embassy."[56] And in a famous spy story from the beginning of the twentieth century, the narrator says of a lady that she was "appealing to my honour so to act that we three should never meet again."[57] I suspect, however, that in both these instances honor is personified. By way of contrast, here are two more quotations, also from the Edwardian era:

> Vanessa Pennington had a husband who was poor, with few redeeming circumstances, and an admirer who, though comfortably rich, was cumbered with a sense of honour. His wealth made him welcome in Vanessa's eyes, but his code of what was right impelled him to go away and forget her, or at the most to think of her in the intervals of doing a great many other things.[58]

> A conventional sense of honour withheld me from disclosing the information I might have given about the young lady.[59]

It seems to me that in these passages—perhaps more clearly in the first than in the second—the words 'a sense of honor' could not properly be replaced by 'honor', and I suspect that, at least by the late nineteenth

55. Barber 1957 records occurrences in 1664 (p. 247), 1667 (p. 243), 1668 (p. 244), 1670 (p. 215), and 1672 (p. 251). The phrase may have been in use much earlier, since Barber has no material for the years 1642–61.

56. Arthur Conan Doyle, *The Adventure of the Gold Pince-Nez*, first published in 1904, and later included in *The Return of Sherlock Holmes*.

57. Erskine Childers, *The Riddle of the Sands* (first published in 1903); see chapter 24, *Finesse*, near the beginning.

58. These are the opening sentences of the story *Cross Currents* by Saki (H. H. Munro). The story is contained in the volume *Reginald in Russia* (first published in 1910; the story itself must have been published in a magazine a little earlier).

59. E. Œ. Somerville and Martin Ross, *The Last Day of Shraft*. The story appears in *Further Experiences of an Irish R.M.*, which was first published in 1908.

century, if 'honor' was used to mean 'sense of honor', then it was only in figurative language.

I assume—again without real evidence—that the kind of transition that I have postulated for English occurred also in other European languages. Thus we find, for instance, in article 12 of the eighteenth-century Spanish *Órdenes Generales para Oficiales* that "the officer whose own honor and spirit do not always stimulate him to perform well is worth very little to the service" (*el oficial cuyo proprio honor y espíritu no le estimulen a obrar siempre bein vale muy poco para el servicio*). In contrast, article 29 of the corresponding orders of 1978 reads as follows: "The sentiment of honor, inspired by a clear conscience, will lead the soldier to the most faithful fulfillment of his duty" (*El sentimiento del honor, inspirado en una recta conciencia, llevará al militar al más exacto cumplimiento del deber*).[60] I believe that 'honor' in the old order is used in the same sense as 'sentiment of honor' in the modern one, and that in both instances what is meant is what we would nowadays call in English the 'sense of honor'.

Let me now summarize the main changes so far mentioned that occur in the notion of honor between roughly the twelfth and the nineteenth century. First, honor comes increasingly to be based on moral virtues. This point is accepted by virtually all students of the subject, and there seems to be no reason to dispute it. Second, it is also generally agreed that honor comes to be more internal. But there is a difference between the way this second change is viewed by followers of the bipartite theory (such as Maurer and Barber) and the way that it is presented here. They believe that 'honor' is used more and more often to refer to a character trait, that is, in a naturally internal sense. I accept that in the early modern period 'honor' was sometimes used in this way, but I believe that this line of development was a dead end. If 'honor' was used in a naturally internal sense to refer to nonmoral qualities (e.g., virility), then such usage became obsolete. Its use in a naturally internal sense to refer to moral qualities may have continued on a limited scale into modern times, but I suggest that in general this usage of the word was displaced by phrases such as 'sense of honor'. The main line of development, I believe, was in the direction of using 'honor' to

60. These two quotations are taken from Pitarch 1984, 55, 57. Circumstances made it impossible for me to check the original sources.

refer to a right, and this, in my view, is a third change that can be observed. 'Honor' was certainly sometimes used to refer to a right in the late Middle Ages,[61] and this sense was at least adumbrated in the high Middle Ages.[62] The internal uses of the word are increasingly cases where it refers to a right, but with attention turned to that which gives the bearer a title to the right.

THE COLLAPSE OF HONOR

It was implied in the section before the last that in modern times the thing that makes one worthy of honor (i.e., honorable) is increasingly the possession of a well-developed sense of honor. This is not to say that other qualifications disappear entirely, but I take it that they become more and more subordinate to the sense of honor. So, for instance, instead of the mere possession of wealth and high social status conferring honor, it is felt rather that it is, say, wealth that gives a man the independence that is necessary if he is to behave in an honorable fashion, and high social status that ensures that he is brought up in such a way that the honor code becomes a part of his very nature. Similarly, I assume that it comes more and more to be felt that to behave in accordance with the code of honor does not, strictly speaking, prove that the man who does so is honorable (though it will no doubt suffice to preserve his honor);[63] what matters is the possession of a well-developed sense of honor, and while a record of behavior in accordance with the code makes it likely that a man possesses such a sense of honor, people can still easily conceive the possibility of a person who acts in accordance with the code for the wrong motives, or of one who violates—or seems to violate—the code for the right motives, uncommon though such cases may be in actuality.

I take the *sense of honor* to be made up of at least two closely related elements: an understanding of what constitutes honorable behavior, and an attachment to such behavior.

This may seem an unnecessarily elaborate definition. For instance, one might be tempted to say that honorableness is simply a combination of whatever virtues are looked on as being indispensable to honor, for example, honesty and courage. The problem with this approach is

61. See the discussion of the guarantee in chapter 8.
62. See the discussion of the passage from *Iwein* at the beginning of this chapter.
63. Barber 1957, 134–35 gives some examples of those who are not really honorable yet retain honor (he classifies them as Ro and Rco).

that honor (of the kind that concerns us here) depends on observing certain rules (the code of honor). In order to follow the code punctiliously it may be necessary to be honest and brave, but it will not be sufficient: one still needs to understand the rules and one still needs a motive for behaving in accordance with them.

In fact even a definition in terms of two elements may be inadequate. One can imagine a man who understands, in a particular situation, what the honorable course of action would be, and who would very much like to follow this course of action, but who finds that he is unable to do so. We can stipulate a variety of things that might prevent him: a pathological fear of heights, inability to stand up to someone who has a much stronger character than himself, overwhelming temptation. Whether, after a man has acted dishonorably for one of these reasons, we could continue to say of him that he has a strong sense of honor depends, of course, on the exact circumstances of the case: if a man whose behavior is otherwise always impeccable fails on a single occasion to do the right thing because of a pathological fear of heights we would surely not see this as evidence of a defective sense of honor; but if someone invariably gives way when he should not to the many people who have stronger characters than himself we may have serious doubts about calling him honorable; and if a man betrays the trust of his best friend in seducing the friend's minor daughter, then we might deny that he has a strong sense of honor, even if his behavior in other spheres of life is impeccable.

It may be then that in order for us to say of a man that he has a well-developed sense of honor it is not enough that he should understand the code of honor and be attached to it: he must perhaps also have the various character traits—courage, self-control, honesty, and the like—that are necessary to ensure that his attachment to the code always—or very nearly always—finds expression in his behavior.

Once the shift is made from basing honor on a certain kind of behavior (always winning in battle, always keeping one's promise) or on the possession of certain external qualities (wealth, health, high rank) to basing it on the possession of certain mostly moral qualities (the ones that we refer to compendiously as the sense of honor), then the way is open for the whole notion of honor to be undermined. Imagine a German army officer of a hundred years ago who is challenged to a duel. He declines the challenge because he is a devout Catholic, and the church strongly condemns dueling. Now for the honor code to be really effective, the officer must be treated as having acted dishonorably. Yet people may find it difficult to do so, since they are sure (we will assume) that he acted as he did not out of cowardice but because of attachment to his faith. They are convinced (we will further assume) that he is profoundly committed to everything in the honor code that is not incompatible with his religious beliefs. In these circumstances people may well feel it appropriate to say of him that he has a strong sense of honor; even if they do not, they will have to admit that he is a man of integrity, and having said this they will find it hard to say that because of his refusal to accept the challenge their respect for him is much diminished. And if the loss of his right to respect is not accompanied by any actual loss of respect, then the honor that is assigned by the honor code has been emptied of its primary content.

I do not want to imply that the introduction of the notion of the sense of honor necessarily leads to a collapse of the notion of honor. The sense of honor was already important in England in the mid–seventeenth century, yet the notion of honor remained alive and well long afterwards. One thing that may have helped to preserve it is intolerance. In order for the Catholic officer in our imaginary example to retain the respect of his non-Catholic fellow officers, the non-Catholics must probably have a certain degree of tolerance, even respect, for the Catholic faith. If the non-Catholics looked on Catholicism in the way that some Protestants did in the sixteenth or seventeenth century—that is, with something like the same degree of abhorrence that we might feel towards Communism or towards National Socialism—then the scenario that we have sketched will not be followed.

I also do not want to imply by the example of the Catholic officer that the sense of honor could only have a dissolving effect on honor in societies that include groups of people holding substantially different ideas as to what constitutes proper behavior. For even in a homogeneous community there can be differences between individuals: in a certain situation, A behaves in a way that he feels is consistent with his honor, whereas B knows that, placed in the same situation, he himself would not have felt that such behavior was consistent with his honor. How does B judge A? Not necessarily as having lost honor: the notion of the sense of honor gives B a concept that helps—indeed encourages—him to look behind A's behavior and judge him rather by his motives.[64]

One position to which emphasizing the sense of honor can lead is illustrated by a letter that appeared in the *New York Times* early in 1992. At the time questions were being raised about the way in which Bill Clinton, later that year elected President of the United States, avoided military service during the Vietnam War. The writer of the letter, Anne Trowbridge, says:

> The concept of personal honor provides me with rules and language for evaluating responses to the Vietnam War. Those I consider honorable:
>
> Conscientious objectors, who endured hardship rather than violate their code of nonviolence; those who, grieving for a society they felt had lost its values, withdrew and went elsewhere; those who, realizing that others would go in their places if they did not, served in the military even if they had deep reservations about the war; those who supported the war and served because they felt it was their duty; others, men and women, who devoted much of their lives to presenting rational and moral arguments against the war, and yet others who felt an authentic call into the ministry or religious life and who have faithfully served in that way.
>
> All of these were operating from strong moral principles, doing what they felt was right, whatever the sacrifices and risks to themselves. They do not all need to agree with one another to be honorable people [. . .]
>
> But there is another group of men to consider [. . .] They felt, and feel, that they have a right to consider only their own short-term preferences [. . .] They do not speak the language of personal honor, but rather of being comfortable, of having the right to eliminate what makes them uncomfortable or what threatens them.
>
> [. . .] During the Vietnam War, some men felt it was their right [. . .] to manipulate the system for their immediate needs and wishes, with no consideration of long-term effects, personal or social.
>
> It is this last group whom we should emphatically reject as national leaders. These people, unmotivated by any sense of personal honor, are crazy-makers in our social life. Since in their thoughts and actions they appeal to no coherent moral world view, their personalities are incoherent too, and their actions unpredictable, how-

64. See further appendix 2 below.

ever good a front they may have constructed to conceal their real selves.[65]

Trowbridge evidently feels that to be honorable is to have a set of values, to draw honest conclusions from those values in a given situation as it is known to one, and then to act in accordance with those conclusions, even when the action is difficult for one. Within broad limits at least, she does not care what one's values are. It may be then that what Trowbridge calls "personal honor" is what would more commonly be called 'integrity'.[66] Alternatively, it is possible that she would say that it is the integrity of certain people that *makes* them honorable, where 'honorable' means something like 'worthy of respect' or 'having a right to respect'. Under this view—which I shall refer to as the *integrity position*—the honor code is reduced to something like the maxim "To thine own self be true" (though with various constraints on the kind of self one may be). Or looking at it in a different way, one can say that almost any set of values that one holds dear counts as one's honor code, and that one's title to honor is the possession of a proper sense of honor.

Many people would probably assent to the integrity position, and yet this fact has little social significance. In substance, the integrity position reduces honor to a virtue, and there is no obvious reason why one would wish to pick out this particular virtue from among various others. It would therefore be surprising if it were the subject of special institutions. This suggests a connection between the collapse of honor institutions in the West and the stress that was increasingly placed on the sense of honor.

Another way in which emphasis on the sense of honor undermines the whole notion of honor can be illustrated with a passage from a speech by Bismarck. He was reacting with characteristic disdain to a statement to the effect that honors had been lavished on him. He said, "Gentlemen, my honor lies in no-one's hand but my own, and it is not something that others can lavish on me; my own honor, which I carry in my heart, suffices me entirely, and no-one is judge of it and able to

65. *New York Times*, February 24, 1992, p. 18A.

66. Compare Collins's account of honor quoted in chapter 2 above, n. 37. The connection between honor and integrity seems to be old: Fielding (1974, 1:55) writes of Jenny Jones that she refused to "forfeit her Honour, or Integrity, by betraying another" (*Tom Jones*, book 1, end of chapter 8).

decide whether I have it. My honor before God and men is my property, I give myself as much as I believe that I have deserved, and I renounce any extra."[67] These words have frequently been quoted as a characteristic expression of inner honor,[68] but it does not seem to have been remarked that, as well as being highly suggestive, they are also remarkably obscure. They seem indeed to defy word-by-word explication. The central problem is perhaps that two very different senses of the word 'honor', those exemplified in the phrases 'it was a great honor' and 'my honor is at stake', are not clearly distinguished. Bismarck is probably claiming that only he himself is able to judge how much respect and esteem he deserves; he implies that the only respect that really matters to him is his self-respect,[69] and perhaps also that whatever it is that makes him worthy of respect comes from within himself, and is not given to him by others.

What does Bismarck mean by the first of these claims? One possibility is that he assigns respect or esteem according to idiosyncratic rules known only to himself (in which case he might also claim that he alone is judge of whether others have honor). A proud man might, for instance, set himself (but not necessarily others) very high standards: he might feel dishonored if he were to behave in a certain way even when others do not view him as being dishonored by such behavior. His self-respect, that is, his right to respect in his own eyes, depends on his following his personal code.

It is more likely, however, that Bismarck is accepting something like the integrity position, and that he is protesting against the idea that others might be able to judge, on the basis only of his words or deeds, to what extent he deserves to be treated with respect or esteem; his point being that one's right to respect does not depend on such externals alone, but rather on the relationship between them and certain

---

67. *Meine Herren, meine Ehre steht in niemandes Hand als in meiner eigenen, und man kann mich damit nicht überhäufen; die eigene, die ich in meinem Herzen trage, genügt mir vollständig, und niemand ist Richter darüber und kann entscheiden, ob ich sie habe. Meine Ehre vor Gott und den Menschen ist mein Eigentum, ich gebe mir selbst so viel, wie ich davon glaube verdient zu haben, und verzichte auf jede Zugabe.* From a speech delivered on November 18, 1881 (Bismarck 1929, 279).

68. For instance, Maurer 1970, 243; Jones 1959, 155; Reiner 1956, 49.

69. This idea is clearly expressed in a sentence that is ascribed to Bismarck (Maurer 1970, 243), but of which I have not traced the source: "I can do without anyone's respect—except my own" (*Ich kann die Achtung aller Menschen entbehren, nur meine eigene nicht*).

internals, notably motives. Since he alone has certain knowledge of these internals, he alone knows for sure whether he really deserves to be honored, and whether he is a man of honor. The same considerations would presumably apply to at least a significant number of Bismarck's fellow beings, so that under this theory it is commonly impossible for the world to know for sure whether someone is or is not a person of honor.

There is no need here to try to evaluate this particular line of reasoning; what matters is that its conclusion was widely accepted by Bismarck's contemporaries. A man's honor was identified with (or seen as founded on) his true worth; his true worth was in turn seen as being based on the possession of certain moral qualities, among which integrity was prominent; and it was concluded that this being so, it is difficult to be certain whether a man has honor or not.[70] Such a view is clearly inimical to social institutions that treat people very differently according to whether they have honor or not; and the existence of this view was one of the reasons why German jurists—who considered themselves forced by the social and legal system to operate with the notion of honor—found it necessary to create complex theories which, like that of Liepmann, distinguished between a man's true honor (which no merely human court of law could safely judge) and certain interests deriving from his honor that the law *could* reasonably hope to protect.

70. So, for instance, one of the most distinguished jurists of the time, after observing that there were many gradations of honor, from the lowest to the highest, wrote that "this scale is not only determined by a person's outward behavior, but above all by the person's character, by their inner life; that is what determines it—the recognition of others is of no significance here" (*diese Stufenleiter wird nicht nur durch das bestimmt, was der Mensch nach aussen thut, sie wird vor allem bestimmt durch seine Gesinnung, sie wird bestimmt durch sein Innenleben; dadurch wird sie bestimmt,—die Anerkennung Dritter ist hier völlig unerheblich*) (Kohler 1900, 2). Kohler denied, of course, that an insult could harm a person's honor.

4

Horizontal and Vertical Honor

Up to now we have been concerned with what I have called *personal honor*. At this point I want to characterize personal honor a little more precisely and to contrast it with some other kinds of honor.

Personal honor was originally described roughly as a right to respect. To this may now be added that the respect in question is of the kind that is due to an equal (in contrast, for instance, to the respect to which a father, in many societies, has a right from his children). I shall refer to any right to this kind of respect as an instance of *horizontal honor*.

Personal honor is a particular type of horizontal honor. Two features have already been mentioned that distinguish it from other types: first, that the right is one that can be lost, and second, that in order to retain it one must follow certain rules, or maintain certain standards, referred to as the code of honor. If the penalty for breaking the rules is not loss of honor, then the rules do not constitute a code of honor.

I shall use the term *honor group*[1] to refer to a set of people who follow the same code of honor and who recognize each other as doing so.[2] Another possible way of defining the *honor right*[3] would be to say that it is the right to be treated as a full or equal member of the honor group.[4] In some ways this may be a better characterization of the honor right than the one given above. The present work does not, however, attempt to analyze the honor right in any precise fash-

1. I take this term from Taylor (1985, 55), though I am perhaps using it in a sense somewhat different from hers.
2. For a profound and original account of how a group may be constituted by something like the general endorsement of a code, see Gilbert 1992, especially 204–36.
3. I use this term to refer to the right to whatever it is that personal honor is a right to. Personal honor has features which are additional to (i.e., not entailed by) the honor right, for instance, losability.
4. This definition would demand some changes in the structure of the model. Instead of starting with the notion of honor it would have to start by establishing the notion of a group of people who follow the same code, and then define personal honor as the right to be treated as a full or equal member of this group.

ion, and so I shall not weigh up the pros and cons of these two approaches.

A model of personal honor must somehow capture the fact that the code of honor is not just any set of rules or standards. Sir Walter Elliot (in Jane Austen's *Persuasion*) is, let us say, widely recognized to be both foolish and absurdly vain, but while many may laugh at him behind his back, he is still able to move in the best circles; if, however, he were to renege on a gambling debt, or if he were to elope with the wife of a fellow baronet, it might be a different matter. The code of honor is a set of standards that has been picked out as having particular importance, that measures an individual's worth along some profoundly significant dimensions; and a member of the honor group who fails to met these standards is viewed not just as inferior but often also as despicable.

A further feature that should be added to the model of personal honor is suggested by a consideration of Roman ideas about honor.

Roman citizens who conducted themselves properly—or at any rate, discreetly—were said to enjoy *fama* 'a good reputation' and *existimatio.* The latter was defined by Callistratus in the late second or early third century A.D. as "the state of unimpaired dignity approved by law and custom" (*existimatio est dignitatis inlaesae status, legibus ac moribus comprobatus*).[5] When these possessions were damaged, the citizen suffered *infamia.* 'Infamy' was a term that covered many types of disgrace, and one who suffered it might face not only social but also legal consequences.[6] The legal sources therefore mention various kinds of people who are considered infamous, among them men who had voluntarily taken a passive role in a homosexual relationship, those condemned in a capital charge, and those hired to fight wild animals as a public spectacle; those dishonorably discharged from the army, actors,

5. *Digest* 50.13.5.1. All references to the Digest of Justinian are to the edition of Mommsen and Krüger as reproduced in Watson 1985, henceforth referred to as *Digest.* The English translation of this passage is based on the one by Berger (1953, 464), but modified in accordance with suggestions from Margaret Gilbert and Alan Watson. On the work from which the quotation is taken, see Kaser 1956, 265–66; on *existimatio* in the legal sources, see Kaser 1956, 231, 274 (who also gives references to *dignitas* used in the same sense).

6. In the discussion that follows of Roman ideas, all references, unless there is an explicit statement to the contrary, are to men. The legal status of women differed in significant respects; for instance, women were debarred from public office.

brothel keepers, those convicted of certain crimes; and also those who had been successfully sued in the civil courts in certain actions, notably theft, fraud, and various kinds of breach of faith or of trust.[7]

These examples are taken from a part of the law that deals with restrictions on the right to postulate, that is, "to set out one's own claim or that of one's friend in court before the presiding officer, or to oppose the claim of another."[8] Various types of infamous people also suffered limitations of other kinds, for example, on their right to serve as decurions (i.e., as members of a city council), as judges, as witnesses, and so on.[9]

Can we infer from this that the Romans had personal honor? In our model such honor is a *single* right that belongs to one who meets a certain set of standards, and that is lost when one fails to meet these standards. If this is so, then what we find in Roman law is not personal honor. For in it different types of infamy might entail the loss of different rights; thus, one who was hired to fight wild animals as a public spectacle was allowed to postulate for himself, but for no one else at all; a brothel keeper, in contrast, though he still did not enjoy the unrestricted right to postulate for others that belonged to a normal citizen, was allowed to postulate both for himself and for certain close others, e.g., relatives.

But the law is not a simple reflection of how ordinary people think about their world, and *existimatio, dignitas, fama,* and their opposite *infamia* were not technical terms of the law;[10] they represent rather notions from ordinary life that were relevant in certain parts of the law. It can be inferred both from the legal material and from other sources that the normal citizen had a right to respect that was diminished or destroyed by any of the numerous forms of infamy mentioned in the law (as well as by others not so mentioned); but it seems to me unlikely that anyone except the lawyers found it necessary to make the fine dis-

7. *Digest* 3.1.1. Watson 1963, 76–85 argues, however, that in classical Roman law a defendant in the civil court could always avoid infamy by appointing someone to represent him in court.

8. *Digest* 3.1.1.2. Unless otherwise indicated, all translations from the *Digest* are taken from Watson 1985.

9. Kaser 1956, 235–44, 255–56, 261–62.

10. At least not of classical Roman law (Kaser 1956, 231); *infamia,* however, develops in this direction in the later law. (For the medieval history of infamy, see Peters 1990.) *Ignominia,* in contrast, was a technical term (Kaser 1956, 227).

tinction between the infamy of a hired animal fighter and the infamy of a brothel keeper. I take it—though this is admittedly no more than a guess—that for the general body of citizens there was broadly speaking merely a distinction between the respectable and the despicable, and that the various neat gradations of infamy that appear in this or that part of the law are more the work of the jurists than a reflection of clearly formed popular ideas on the subject.

Given this, then the Romans had all the components of personal honor that are listed at the beginning of this chapter. But there is another question that I think we must ask: did the Romans also regularly refer to precisely the right to respect of the respectable? This is practically the same as asking whether they had a word or phrase that referred to personal honor. The answer to this question is not entirely clear to me. The Romans had many words in the same semantic region as 'honor',[11] and some of them are in certain occurrences translated as 'honor': thus *fides* and *honestas* among words that seem to relate mainly to the personal qualities of the individual, and *dignitas* and *existimatio* among words that seem to relate mainly to how the individual is viewed by others. *Existimatio* is especially interesting. It was evidently thought of as something that could be preserved, lost, diminished, or restored, but not as something that could be increased. Callistratus, after giving the definition cited above, proceeds to describe how *existimatio* may be diminished or destroyed; the other occurrences in the legal sources are of the same kind;[12] and in the literature of the late Republic one repeatedly reads of *existimatio* being damaged or lost in one way or another,[13] but not apparently of it being built up or growing. Perhaps 'good name' is the English term that comes closest to translating the word when it is used in the late Republican sources in

11. Oppermann 1983 offers a useful, though now somewhat outdated, guide to the literature on several of the relevant terms (among them *fides, dignitas*, and *honor*, though there is nothing on some other important words, e.g., *pudor* and *honestas*). Although there are admirable lexical investigations of such terms, there is much less about how they are related to each other, and there seems to be no comprehensive (i.e., conceptual) discussion of Roman notions of honor. It is also striking that many of the authors who analyze the use of these terms pay little attention to the legal sources. (For *fides*, see now the extensive bibliography in Nörr 1989, 102.)

12. See especially the *Vocabularium iurisprudentiae romanae*, s.v. *"existimatio."*

13. For example, *existimationem lacerare, violare, perdere, offendere;* Yavetz 1974, 37, 45.

a positive sense (for one can, though less commonly, also have a bad *existimatio*). It is something that one attempts to preserve and defend rather than to gain. In all this it resembles the kind of honor that most interests us in this essay. Nevertheless, both in Callistratus's definition and elsewhere *existimatio* seems to be that which gives one a title to a right rather than the right itself.[14]

I will leave it to those better qualified than I am to decide what words, if any, were used by the Romans to refer precisely to a right to the respect enjoyed by the normal citizen. This much at least seems to me almost certain: that there was no word or phrase that was *frequently* used in the sense that interests us. So while individuals were undoubtedly conscious of having the rights that went with undamaged standing in the community, and undoubtedly attached great importance to them, they probably did not regularly refer to them as such. To say, for instance, of a man that his *existimatio* was intact or that he had done nothing to bring *ignominia* upon himself would imply with all the necessary clarity that he possessed the rights that went with this happy state.

In what follows I shall confine the use of the term *personal honor* to those groups that *do* have at least one word or phrase that is frequently used to refer to this honor. By this I do not mean that the word or phrase must be frequently used, but rather that when it is used, then it refers in a substantial proportion of its occurrences to just this right. This is the last feature to be mentioned here that distinguishes personal honor from other kinds of horizontal honor. The notion of personal honor as it is used here implies therefore not only a particular social structure but also that the language of those in that structure indicates that they view the structure in a particular way. The Romans, as it happens, did not look at their structure in this way.

In chapter 1 a distinction was drawn between descriptive studies of honor that are conceptual in their approach and those that are lexical. The implication of the previous paragraph is that if a society does have personal honor, then the notion as it exists in that society can only properly be described by paying careful attention to the way that mem-

---

14. This accords with the interpretation of the term given by Ihering. He called *existimatio* "the Roman technical term for honor [*Ehre*] in the sense in which the term is used in private law" (Ihering 1898, 2:500). Ihering (1898, 2:496, 501) defined honor as "the worth of the person" (*der Wert der Person*) or more specifically as "the worth of a person in law" (*der Rechtswert der Person*).

bers of the society use certain words or phrases. In other words, what is essentially a lexical approach is called for.

Although the respect to which one has a right by virtue of possessing horizontal honor can be lost, it cannot be increased (since if one has a right to more respect than others, then the right is no longer to the respect that is due to an equal); and for this reason it is sometimes referred to as 'negative honor'. Horizontal honor may be contrasted with *vertical* (or positive) *honor,* the right to special respect enjoyed by those who are superior, whether by virtue of their abilities, their rank, their services to the community, their sex, their kin relationship, their office, or anything else.[15] Of the many types of vertical honor, the most familiar to us is perhaps *rank honor,* that is, the honor that is enjoyed by all members of a superior rank in relations with their inferiors. Inferiors are naturally put firmly in their place if they fail to manifest this respect. More interestingly, members of the superior class may be forbidden by the honor code to waive their right to respect. A. N. Gilbert, in examining cases in the British army of the eighteenth century of "conduct unbecoming an officer and a gentleman," discovered a number of instances where the conduct in question consisted of undue familiarity with the rank and file. In 1760, for instance, an ensign was accused, among other things, of drinking with the private soldiers. He admitted the fact, but said in his defense that "the Men continued to preserve that respect which is due to an officer." Despite this, the ensign was found guilty. Gilbert classifies offenses of this sort as honor crimes, and indeed the ensign in question was forced to ask the pardon of his entire battalion "for the Dishonour this my Behaviour may have reflected on them."[16]

Another important type of vertical honor is what may be called *competitive honor,* the honor that is enjoyed by those who have shown

15. The terms 'horizontal honor' and 'vertical honor' are taken from Correa 1958. Barber (1985, 13; 1957, 127–32) refers to these (or, at any rate, something similar) as "negative honour" and "positive honour" (or "reputation") respectively. Schopenhauer also notes the negative character of the kind of honor one is liable to lose (n.d., 60). Pitt-Rivers (1977, 31, 36, 38, 42), in making much the same distinction, uses the terms 'honor = virtue' and 'honor = precedence' (cf. Gilmore 1987, 5–6; it should be added perhaps that Pitt-Rivers, 1977, 20, 38, 42, also has an 'honor = shame'). As Barber (1957, 127) points out, the distinction between the two types of honor had already been made at least as far back as the sixteenth century.

16. Gilbert 1976, 86.

themselves to be superior as individuals.[17] Those who had *êre* in the German Arthurian romances seem often to have had this kind of honor, and it is also the type of honor that was associated with the classical Greek *timē*. Aristotle said that "the components of *timē* are sacrifices, memorials in verse and prose, privileges, grants of land, front seats, public burial, State maintenance, and among the barbarians, prostration and giving place, and such gifts as are valued in the particular country where they are made."[18] *Timē* was translated into Latin as *honor*, and so English translations of Aristotle also generally render it as 'honor'. Aristotle evidently understands the word here as referring to the manifestations of special respect, but it had a wide range of other, though related, meanings.[19]

Like *timē*, the Latin word *honor* had many uses, but all in the context of vertical relations. On occasion, at least, it may mean precisely the right to special respect that arises from superior rank. Consider the following passage from Marcian (towards the middle of the third century A.D.): "Veterans and their children have the same *honor* as decurions: accordingly, they shall not be condemned to the mines, nor to forced labor, or to the beasts, and they are not beaten with rods."[20] *Honor* here probably does not mean "prestige" or the "esteem which attaches to a member of the higher orders":[21] the mere fact (if indeed it was one) that veterans and their offspring *enjoyed* the same esteem as decurions would not entail that they had a *right* to such esteem. Thus a woman may find that because of her beauty she is treated as being of special value, without anyone, including herself, believing that her beauty gives her a *right* to such treatment. In this passage the word

17. Cf. Finley 1977, 118: "It is the nature of honour that it must be exclusive, or at least hierarchic. When everyone attains equal honour, then there is no honour for anyone. Of necessity, therefore, the world of Odysseus was fiercely competitive, as each hero strove to outdo the others."
    18. *Rhetoric* I.v.9. The translation is that of J. H. Freese (Aristotle 1926), apart from the last phrase, which is taken from another translation, the reference to which I no longer have.
    19. There is a large body of scholarship on the notion of honor as it appears in the Homeric poems (see, for instance, Riedinger 1976 and Ulf 1990); but *timē* and related terms (e.g., *doxa* and *kudos*) as they are used in later ancient Greek literature have not received the attention they deserve. See meanwhile Greindl 1940 and Lloyd-Jones 1990; Cairns 1993 also contains much valuable material, including an extensive bibliography.
    20. *Digest* 49.18.3.
    21. As suggested by Garnsey (1970, 2 n, 223, 258; cf. 246).

"accordingly" (*igitur*) suggests either a right or something that gives title to a right, that is, standing or rank.[22] The possible interpretations are in fact much the same as those suggested for *ère* in the passage from *Iwein* quoted in chapter 3.

Vertical and horizontal honor are of course compatible with each other. One kind of relationship that can exist between different types of honor is illustrated by the story of the unfortunate ensign, for it is the code of horizontal honor that forbids him to waive his vertical honor. And it would seem—if we can summarize what was no doubt a complex reality in a schematic fashion—that his right to the vertical respect depended on his right to the horizontal respect: if he was no longer recognized by the other officers and gentlemen as one of their number, then he no longer had a right to the relevant kind of respect from the men (though he might have continued to receive it).

In this instance I assume that horizontal and vertical honor are always congruent with each other; but from a purely logical point of view this need not be so. We can imagine that all the members of the upper class regard X as their equal, but that the members of the lower class refuse to treat him as their superior; or that the members of the lower class regard Y as superior, but the members of the upper class refuse to treat him as an equal. In the real world, of course, a fair degree of congruence is to be expected—and the upper class is much more likely it get its way than is the lower class.

The interaction of horizontal and vertical honor in a particular case can be illustrated by an ordinance published by the rectors of the city of Brescia in the year 1589. The document begins by noting that there have been a number of homicides—obviously in duels—simply as a result of quarrels about precedence on the street; and it goes on to rule that in order to maintain the peace, when two gentlemen meet in the street, the one who is walking with the wall immediately to his right must not be forced to abandon his position. Those who disobey are threatened with exile, imprisonment, corporal punishment, and fines.[23] Duels over matters of precedence—including just this type of precedence—were in fact common in many parts of early modern Eu-

22. The translator of this passage from the *Digest* in Watson 1985 chooses the second possibility, and renders *honor* as "honorable status."
23. Livi 1899, 739.

rope.[24] In such a conflict one party at least was claiming to be superior to the other; but despite the claim to superiority in one dimension, there was a recognition of equality in another, since a gentleman would fight a duel only with another gentleman.

The same thing can be seen from a different angle in a letter written by John Wilkes in 1762. Wilkes is describing what he said to Lord Talbot, a man who held himself to have been insulted by an anonymous piece that had appeared in the *North Briton,* and who demanded to know whether Wilkes was its author: "I observed that I was a private English gentleman, perfectly free and independent, which I held to be a character of the highest dignity; that I obeyed with pleasure a gracious sovereign, but would never submit to the arbitrary dictates of a fellow-subject, a Lord Steward of his household; my superior indeed in rank, fortune, and abilities, but my equal only in honour, courage, and liberty."[25] Wilkes, in contrast to the Brescian duelists, admits that along certain important dimensions he is inferior to his opponent. By our definition the inferiority in these two examples—acknowledged in one, disputed in the other—involves vertical honor: one at least of the Brescians is claiming the right to a kind of respectful behavior that is due only to a superior, and Wilkes would surely have acknowledged that Talbot's rank made it a duty for Wilkes to treat him in certain circumstances with the respect due to a superior.

Would the actors themselves have used the words 'honor' in this context? I believe that Wilkes would have agreed that he owed Lord Talbot the honor that was due from a commoner to a peer of the realm and a Lord Steward; and I suspect that the Brescian duelists would have accepted both that they were in one sense equal in honor and that in another sense one at least of them was claiming to be superior in honor.

The definition of vertical honor given here does not reflect a common use—in fact, may not reflect any use—of the word 'honor' in the major modern European languages. In itself this is not a reason to reject the definition; but if the definition does not give us any new insight into the use of the word 'honor', then it has to justify itself solely by

---

24. See, for instance, Billacois 1986, 128, 131 (France) and Barber 1957, 140 (England).

25. Postgate 1929, 44. Note the characteristically 'equivocal' use of the word 'honor' here: it can be taken in either an external or an internal sense.

virtue of its usefulness in analyzing social structure. I am by no means certain that it can do so. The implication of the definitions given here of horizontal honor and of vertical honor is that almost all rights to respect are honor (to cover the whole field one would also have to consider the right to respect that an inferior may have in relation to a superior). This may well not be a sensible categorization, and certainly this essay does not pretend to deal with anything like so large a subject matter. In what follows, 'honor' will generally mean horizontal honor, specifically, personal honor. This is the honor that has been most prominent in the West since about the seventeenth century, and this is the honor that has attracted most of the attention in the literature on the subject.

Although the definitions of vertical honor and of horizontal honor given here are more or less unsatisfactory, it does seem to me—as it has to many others—that a distinction between two kinds of honor along something like these lines is necessary. On the one hand, a complete separation is not possible. I do not think it is a matter of chance that the word 'honor' in the major modern European languages covers both vertical and horizontal relations. As we shall see, something similar occurs also in Arabic. I take it that the linking of the two types of honor has to do with the fact that behind the notion of honor lie notions like respect and value, which are at least as much in place in relations between unequals as between equals. And on the other hand, the evidence is overwhelming that we cannot simply lump together honor in a vertical and honor in a horizontal context.

5

REFLEXIVE HONOR

Among certain groups the manner in which you react to being treated in a way that you (or others) view as not being consonant with your standing is likely itself to have a profound effect on that standing. This is not *necessarily* the case. Imagine a society in which the highest esteem goes to martial virtues, and in which I am a successful warrior and hence much honored. A jealous rival calls me a coward. I may react by ignoring him completely, by laughing at him, by giving him a cuff over the ear, by throwing back some abusive remark at him, by starting legal proceedings against him, or in some other fashion. But whatever I do, it will generally not affect my right to special respect. At most it may affect my reputation in some other way. Perhaps after the incident people will say of me, "He has earned our respect as a great warrior. Of course, he's a hothead—he should have ignored that idiot who insulted him, and instead he ran after him and cuffed him over the ear. But what does that matter? Look at how he fought our enemies!"

Suppose now that I am an officer in the Austro-Hungarian army at around the turn of the century, and the same thing occurs. *How* I react to this aspersion on my courage will be crucially important to my future standing as a man of honor. Very likely I will have no option but to challenge my rival to a duel. The fact that everyone knows, from my long and distinguished military record, that I am anything but a coward, is neither here nor there. If I fail to issue the challenge (under circumstances where it is generally agreed that I should have issued it) my honor will be shattered (and one probable consequence is that I shall have to resign my commission).

In what follows, this kind of honor will be referred to as *reflexive honor*. What distinguishes it is this: that if A impugns B's honor, then B's honor is ipso facto diminished or destroyed, unless B responds with an appropriate counterattack on A.[1] Rules which govern this matter are part of the code of honor.

---

1. What I have called 'reflexive honor' is in some ways close to what Schopenhauer calls "knightly honor" (*ritterliche Ehre*) or *point d'honneur*.

This is, of course, only a very rough characterization. For instance, there are normally restrictions, sometimes very narrow restrictions, on A's identity: a variety of circumstances may make it permissible, or even obligatory, for B to ignore A's action. Here are some examples from the works of theorists in sixteenth-century Italy.[2] It was agreed that A must not be a woman or child, nor a scholar or cleric, nor socially inferior to B. In these cases, the difficulty is that A does not have honor, or does not have the same kind of honor as B; so we may say that one type of constraint that may exist on the identity of A—and it is a very common one—is that A must belong to the same honor group as B. Another type of constraint that may exist is illustrated by the rule that A may not be B's father or B's son. The reason for this is that father and son have the same honor. A third type of restriction appears in the demand that A not be intoxicated or insane.

Personal honor depends on following the demands of the honor code, which no doubt varies a good deal from one society to another. If the honor is reflexive, however, the possible demands of the code on which it is based are somewhat restricted. It may be a rule that I must attack you if you call me a liar or a coward, but it would be very odd if I were supposed to respond in the same way if you call me unforgiving, cruel, insensitive, lacking in humility, or uncharitable.

Reflexive honor tends to be associated with horizontal rather than vertical honor. This is not so by logical necessity, but there are various factors that tend to make it so. If a superior insults an inferior, then generally speaking the inferior is either going to have to swallow the insult or get his revenge by means other than a direct challenge to the insulter. Rudyard Kipling's story *His Private Honour*[3] illustrates the contrast between how an inferior can (or cannot) deal with an insult and how an equal can do so. A subaltern, a decent but very callow young man, in a moment of anger inadvertently strikes one of his soldiers with his riding cane. The blow—"the merest nervous flick of an exasperated boy"—causes no harm beyond a tear in the soldier's uniform, but the soldier resents it deeply. "After seven years' service and three medals, he had been struck by a boy younger than himself!"

The soldier is so taken aback by the blow that he makes no immediate response, and he subsequently refuses to lodge an official com-

2. What follows is taken from Bryson 1935, 31–33.
3. First published in 1891; collected in the volume *Many Inventions.*

plaint about the subaltern's act. Indeed, he lies to a superior officer in order to conceal it, even though a complaint would in a sense be a highly effective revenge, since it would lead to the subaltern's being cashiered. At the very end of the story the soldier explains why he lied. First, he says, it would not have been fair to destroy the young officer's career because of an inadvertent blow, and second, as a man it was up to him to deal with the matter in person. This view is supported by Mulvaney, a highly respected member of the soldier's circle, when he says that "if he had ha' told on his shuperior orf'cer I'd ha' come out to Fort Amara to kick him into the Fort ditch, an' that's a forty-fut drop."

Mulvaney, however, though he forbids the only kind of response that is legally open to the soldier, does not offer any alternative; he merely says that the fact that it was an officer who struck the blow is irrelevant, that the insult is "between man and man." The soldier feels that the insult can only be wiped out by his own direct action—"I want that young beggar's hide took off" are his words. Because such action seems to be ruled out, a tense and unhappy impasse arises that is strongly felt both by the soldier and by the subaltern; in fact all the men under the young officer's command are demoralized by the event.

Only after much thought does the subaltern see the way out: he creates a situation in which he and the soldier are alone and proposes a fistfight. Both acquit themselves well in the fight, the subaltern apologizes for the original blow, the soldier accepts his apology, and the tension is dissolved.

What has happened is this: the subaltern succeeded eventually in putting the correct interpretation on the fact that the soldier did not complain—he understood that the soldier saw the insult as having been between equals, and so did not want it resolved within the hierarchical structure of the army, where he, the soldier, could act only in the role of an inferior. In thinking this through—in realizing that the soldier did not act as he did out of a wish to be bought off, or because he attached little importance to the blow, or because he simply wanted a personal apology—the subaltern becomes wiser, and when next seen (after the fight) he has acquired a new maturity. Perhaps the subaltern has also had to digest the fact that the soldier, though his inferior in one dimension, is his equal in another. It is at any rate a sign of the striking changes that had taken place in English society since the eighteenth century that an officer can plausibly be portrayed as willing to treat a soldier as an equal in this way.

The other possibility in vertical honor is for an inferior to insult a superior. Honor codes (for instance, the Italian ones mentioned above) often take account of this by providing that insults from inferiors should be—or at least, may be—ignored. One reason for this may be that to take seriously an insult that someone offers is to show that person a certain measure of respect, to put oneself on that person's level. Another may be that it is too easy for the superior to retaliate against the inferior—you do not prove that you are a real man by running through a woman or a child with your rapier. When the code does allow retaliation for an insult from an inferior, then the retaliation may take a disdainful form: an eighteenth-century lord, rather than call out an inferior who had insulted him, might simply send round some servants to beat him up.

Reflexive honor was apparently unknown to the Greeks and Romans.[4] This is not to say that they took insults lightly. In Rome, for instance, affronts of many kinds were actionable as *iniuria*, and "few sections of private law were treated with equal theoretical refinement and practical insight."[5] If we look at the acts that are classified as *iniuria*— everything from the intentional infliction of physical injury, through the publication of defamatory material, to preventing someone from taking his seat in the theater—we will not in general be surprised that they are treated as delicts; but it is remarkable that they are all grouped under the one heading, a heading whose central organizing concept is *contumelia*, 'insult'.[6] The Romans were sensitive about their honor, and various kinds of *iniuria* are explicitly described as pertaining to *dignitas*, or to *existimatio*, or to *ignominia*.[7] Yet there is nothing to suggest that this honor was reflexive: in the long and varied list that can be drawn up from the legal sources of things that made a person infamous, we nowhere find it written that a man brings infamy upon himself if he fails to prosecute (or otherwise retaliate against) another who slapped him in the face, or who wrote epigrams against him, or who

4. Cf. Schopenhauer n.d., 74–76.
5. Mommsen 1899, 790.
6. Wittmann 1974, 290–99; Pólay 1989, 521–22. This is not to say that every single offense classified as an *iniuria* was looked on primarily as an insult; for instance, the wrong done in the intentional infliction of a *serious* physical injury may well have been viewed in a different light.
7. *Digest* 47.10.1.2 and 4.

seduced his wife. Nor is it likely that society had hard-and-fast rules about the matter. Seneca, for instance, in *De constantia,* deals at length with the question of how one should react to injury (*iniuria*) and insult (*contumelia*).[8] The epitome of the aspect of his teaching that concerns us here is that "the wise man [. . .] will never allow himself to pay to the one who offered him an insult the compliment of admitting that it was offered."[9] Now the only difficulties that Seneca sees in following this policy are psychological ones, those of dealing with feelings of anger or humiliation; there is nowhere any indication that to ignore an insult or injury will endanger one's social standing, and indeed Seneca says explicitly of insult (as opposed to injury) that "men are not harmed, but angered by it" (*non laeduntur homines sed offenduntur*).[10]

Among the Germanic peoples, in contrast, reflexive honor may have existed at an early date, and it constitutes the central theme of the Icelandic sagas.[11] It appears equally in a Swedish law of the thirteenth century: if A insults B by accusing him of being unmanly, B should deny the accusation and challenge A to single combat. If B then fails to turn up for the duel, "then he will become what he has been called, and he is not qualified to take an oath, nor is he valid as a witness, either for man or woman."[12] At a much later time reflexive honor is well attested elsewhere on the periphery of Europe, in the Balkans.[13] Reflexive honor appears in a very marked form in Western Europe with the 'point of honor' and the duel, that is, at the time of the Renaissance. Northern Europe learned of the duel, like so much else, from Italy.[14] Eventually the duel spread as far east as Russia and as far west as the

8. Seneca uses the word *iniuria* in a sense different from the one it carries in the technical language of the law. The paradigm of *iniuria* is for Seneca physical injury (section 15.1), though he also includes many other things under this heading, for instance theft and unjust condemnation (as suffered by Socrates) (section 2.3). Neither of the latter would be legal *iniuria,* whereas *contumelia,* which Seneca contrasts to *iniuria,* would often be legal *iniuria.*

9. Seneca 1935, 89 (section 13.5).

10. Seneca 1935, 59 = section 4.3.

11. Gehl 1937, 73.

12. Meulengracht Sørensen 1983, 31.

13. Boehm 1987; Gesemann 1943.

14. See especially the outstanding article by Morel (1964, 632); similarly, Billacois 1986, 40. Erspamer (1982, 44–46) argues that the point of honor actually originated in Spain, though he accepts that it was from Italy that it radiated to the rest of Europe (and was even reexported, in a revised form, to Spain).

New World, and it remained an important feature of life, at least among certain classes in certain parts of the world, until well into the twentieth century.[15]

I mentioned in chapter 3 certain changes that occurred in Western Europe during the transition from high medieval to modern honor. They can be summarized by saying that honor, originally something like prestige, comes increasingly to be a right, and that which gives one title to this right comes increasingly to be certain moral virtues, comprehensively referred to as a sense of honor. Another feature of this same transition has to do with reflexivity. The change has, I think, been widely perceived, but it has yet to be fully and clearly described. It appears, for instance, in Barber's material. Among the various items in the seventeenth-century code of honor he notes "sensitivity to injury and insult" and "insisting on one's rights,"[16] and more generally he speaks of "duelling-honor." This type of honor becomes increasingly prominent in his sources as he tracks its occurrence from the end of the sixteenth to the end of the seventeenth century.[17]

Now as was indicated above, the duel and the point of honor spread through Europe only in the sixteenth century. Can we infer then that the knightly honor of the Middle Ages was not reflexive? Apparently not: "Homicide was [. . .] demanded of [. . .] knights when their honor was impugned [. . .] knights were not allowed to forgive insults,"[18] and "A nobleman reacts to every injury to his honor, which must, in accordance with his rank, be revenged with arms."[19] From Spain we have the legend of Count Garci Fernández, whose wife runs off with another man. He eventually succeeds in decapitating the pair of

15. Frevert 1991 is an invaluable study of the duel in Germany in the nineteenth and twentieth century; unfortunately, nothing equally comprehensive seems to exist for any other European country in this period, or indeed for the Americas. (I have not seen Mironov 1991.) For references to the literature on countries other than Germany, see Frevert 1991, 275 n. 17. Rivanera's code of honor (i.e., handbook of rules for duelists) first appeared in 1954. In 1961 an extended edition was published by the Argentinian army, in which the author was a senior officer dealing with legal matters. This suggests that the duel still retained some importance in military circles at the time.

16. Barber 1957, 140.

17. Barber 1957, 274.

18. Jones 1959, 89.

19. Bosl 1977, 29. Cf. also Robreau 1981, 28: *Le devoir de vengeance [. . .] s'inscrit pleinement dans cette conception particulière de l'honneur qu'offre notre corpus.*

them, gathers his vassals in Burgos, shows them the victims' heads, and says, "Now I am worthy of being your lord, because I am avenged. Previously, when I lived in dishonor, I was not."[20] As for insisting on one's rights, it has been said that one of the most prominent items in the code of honor that is implied by the poems of the troubadours is that "it is a duty of honor for anyone who rules a country boldly to fight for his rights and his interests against enemies, and shameful, in contrast, to allow one's enemies to rob one without making any resistance."[21]

And yet there is a difference. The honor of the Arthurian romances is quite unlike that of the Icelandic sagas. Much of the action in the sagas depends on the extraordinary sensitivity of its characters to any kind of affront. A perfectly sane man may kill another on the spot for making a disrespectful remark.[22] A figure like the Sir Kay of the Arthurian romances, who regularly insults knights and gets away with it, is inconceivable in this world. And the Icelanders have attitudes only slightly more extreme than those that were common among the European aristocracy of the early modern era, or that could be found in the Balkans until at least very recent times. Among the Sarakatsani, for instance, a community of Greek shepherds, it has been said of the typical young man that "it is not only the reality of an obvious insult which provokes him to action, but even the finest of allusions on which it is possible to place some unflattering construction."[23]

Reflexivity, then, seems to be a matter of degree. It may be correct to distinguish between reflexive and nonreflexive systems of honor, but among the reflexive systems there are evidently many shades; and the change that comes into European honor after the Renaissance may be an increased sensitivity to insult rather than a new view of the importance that is attached to reacting properly to insult.

Whatever the ethos of the system as a whole, some men will be quick to see their honor as having been impugned, while others will use every

---

20. In the original: *agora so yo pora seer uuestro sennor que so uengado, ca non mientra estana desonrrado* (Menéndez Pidal 1955, 2:428; the story is summarized, and this quotation translated into modern Spanish, from which I have translated it into English, in Menéndez Pidal 1964, 156–58). The chronicle from which this passage is taken comes from the late thirteenth century; Menéndez Pidal believes that the story is taken from a poem.
21. Settegast 1887, 18.
22. See, for instance, Gehl 1937, 45–51.
23. Campbell 1966, 148.

evasion possible in order to avoid acknowledging that such an impugnment has taken place. Sometimes there is a special form in which a man who seems indifferent to dishonor may be spurred on: someone close to him—very often a woman—will reproach him for his inaction.[24] The point of this seems to be to make it clear to the man that it is not merely the world at large which views him as having lost—or being on the verge of losing—his right to respect, but even his nearest and dearest, those who in most circumstances will support him even when all others fail. Something of the sort may have existed among the Bedouin in ancient times,[25] but there is nothing of the sort nowadays that is specific to ʿird.

24. In Old Norse an incitement of this kind was called a *hvǫt* (Gehl 1937, index s.v.) or *frýja* (Meulengracht Sørensen 1983, index s.v.); very similar is the Corsican *rimbecco* (Busquet 1920, 108–12); see also O'Leary 1987, 27 n. 1, 29–31.
25. Farès 1932, 39 (a man who is reproached by his sister for failing to revenge their late brother), 67 (women are brought to battle and say, "You are not our husbands if you do not defend us").

PART TWO

6

THE MEDITERRANEAN

The anthropologists who brought the importance of honor to the attention of their colleagues almost all worked in countries that border on the Mediterranean, and subsequent anthropological research has also concentrated on this area. Some of the leading investigators have in fact argued that there is a peculiarly Mediterranean notion of honor,[1] and certain anthropologists will write without hesitation of "Mediterranean culture" and "the Mediterranean code of honor and shame."[2] Other scholars have denied that such things exist,[3] while a number take the position that the matter remains to be decided.[4]

The Mediterranean honor theory is based on the observation that there are certain similarities in the notions of honor to be found in various societies that border on the Mediterranean. Now it is undoubtedly true that the peoples of southern Europe, and especially the rural peoples, resemble in some ways those of the Levant and North Africa more than they do those of northern Europe.[5] This is in part because of climatic and geographical similarities, and in part because of his-

1. For instance, Pitt-Rivers 1977:xi (if I understand him correctly, he asserts that there is a Mediterranean honor that can be contrasted with northern European honor); Gilmore 1987b, 16; and Davis 1989, 48. Gilmore 1982 reviews the literature in English that deals with the Mediterranean as a culture area; honor is dealt with on pp. 191–92.
    2. Jowkar 1986, 51, 50.
    3. Most recently Pina-Cabral 1989, to which Gilmore 1990 provides a powerful response.
    4. This seems to be the tenor of the latest pronouncement by Peristiany and Pitt-Rivers (1991b, 6).
    5. The attempts by the Mediterranean honor theorists to characterize these resemblances have not, however, been very happy. Pitt-Rivers (1977:x), for instance, mentions among "the general structural characteristics of the Mediterranean communities: their moral cohesiveness and the absence of the contrast between town and country which was so important in England and northern Europe." I see no reason to believe that "moral cohesiveness," whatever that may be, is or was any more common in (say) Moroccan communities than in Norwegian ones. As for the contrast between town and country, it has long been extremely marked in much of North Africa and the Levant; there is no reason to believe that it is less marked than in northern Europe, and considerable evidence (e.g., from dialectology) that it is more marked.

tory. One relevant historical fact is that much of southern Europe was at one time or another under Muslim rule—a rule that ended, in the case of Sicily, in the eleventh century, in the case of Spain in the fifteenth century, and in the case of the Balkans only in the nineteenth and twentieth centuries, and even then not entirely. The Muslims surely left their stamp on these areas in one way or another.

Yet the theory of Mediterranean honor is not an inherently plausible one. The Mediterranean reached its peak as a unified culture area during the early centuries of the Christian Era; even then its peoples spoke two major languages (Latin in the West and Greek in the East), to say nothing of numerous minor ones; and the cultural unit of which it formed part extended as far north as Britain and as far east as Mesopotamia. Since the early Middle Ages the Mediterranean has been divided between the civilization of Islam and the civilization of Christianity, and until well into the nineteenth century interaction within each civilization was incomparably more intense than interaction between them. There are, I believe, important features that these two civilizations share and that distinguish them from, for instance, the civilizations of East Asia. We would not, however, expect to find a profoundly felt social ideal that is shared by the peoples of the Mediterranean, but not by the Christian world that lies to the north or by the Muslim world that lies to the east and the south. Have the proponents of Mediterranean honor demonstrated that honor is such an ideal?

One thing they would have to do in order to make their case would be to show that ideas of honor in southern Europe, as well as resembling those of other areas of the Mediterranean, differ from those of northern Europe. To the best of my knowledge this has not been attempted.[6]

What may perhaps have misled some scholars is that much of

6. At least not in any systematic fashion. Pitt-Rivers has, however, made an observation that is relevant to this point. He writes that "honor [. . .] is explicitly recognized only in the laws of the countries of southern Europe" (Pitt-Rivers 1968, 509). But this is simply untrue. Honor is, for instance, explicitly mentioned in article 443 of the Belgian penal code (*l'honneur*); in article 261 of the Dutch penal code (*eer*); in the title of chapter 5 of the Swedish penal code (*Om ärekränkning*); in article 267(1) of the Danish penal code (*aere*); in the title of chapter 23 of the Norwegian penal code (*ærekrænkelser*), as well as in most of the articles (246–54) that make up the chapter; in article 131 of the penal code of the Russian Soviet Federated Socialist Republic (*chest'*); and in article 177 of the Swiss penal code (*l'honneur* in the French version that I consulted). And this is by no means a complete list.

southern Europe has in recent centuries changed far more slowly than the rest of the continent. It is therefore in many ways more reasonable to compare, say, Andalusian or Sicilian villagers of the first half of the twentieth century with English or German villagers of two centuries earlier, rather than with the English or German villagers who were their contemporaries.

A second thing the Mediterranean honor theorists would have to do in order to prove their case is to show that ideas of honor in the Muslim countries that border the Mediterranean, as well as resembling those in the southern European countries, differ from those in the Muslim lands to the east and south. This too has not been attempted. One may lay it to the credit of Jane Schneider that she noticed the marked similarities between the Northern Somalis and the Muslims of the Mediterranean basin. Her way of dealing with this, however, which was to describe the Northern Somalis as "culturally part of the Mediterranean,"[7] is not likely to be widely followed. Somaliland is, after all, farther from the Mediterranean than Denmark is. This is not in itself a decisive counterargument (after all, it is not unreasonable to include much of the New World as part of the region of European culture). But if Somaliland is to be annexed to the Mediterranean, then why not also annex Iraq, Iran, Afghanistan, and Pakistan? The truth that lies behind Schneider's assertion is simply that the Somalis are part of the Islamic world, and as such have been profoundly influenced by the Arabs in general, and by the Bedouin in particular.

The primary ethnographic data in this essay come from fieldwork carried out between 1976 and 1982 among the Aḥaywāt, a Bedouin tribe of which some 160 families lived in central Sinai. All of them were at that time nomads. The traditional territory of the tribe lies a couple of hundred kilometers south of the Mediterranean,[8] but their culture is not substantially different from that of the tribes that live in northern Sinai and that hold territory right up to the shore. Many Bedouin could, indeed, like the tribes of northern Sinai, be considered Mediterranean people: the whole long strip of territory that lies to the north of the Sahara has (or had until modern times) an important Arabic-speaking nomadic population whose values and way of life were in

7. Schneider 1971, 7.
8. See Stewart 1986 for a detailed account.

many fundamental respects the same as those of the Aḥaywāt. Yet the great mass of the Bedouin is to be found elsewhere: in the Syrian Desert, in Iraq, in western Iran, and in the Arabian peninsula, with important offshoots in the Sudan and along the southern borders of the Sahara, continuing as far as the Atlantic coast. To say of the Bedouin that they are a Mediterranean people is true only in the same way that it is true to say of the Russians that they are a Pacific people.

I suggest that in the discussion of honor it is never appropriate to treat the peoples who border the Mediterranean as a discrete unit. (In contrast it is, for instance, sometimes appropriate to treat the Icelanders or the English as a discrete unit for this purpose.) Not all peoples living on the shores of the Mediterranean have been affected to the same degree by their proximity to it; and even if we take groups like the Catalans and the Lebanese, who *have* been deeply affected by their relationship to the Mediterranean, this fact does not entail that they should resemble each other more than they resemble their inland neighbors to the north and the east, respectively. For one thing, different human groups can react very differently to similar circumstances; and for another, the fact that people have been deeply influenced by their location does not mean that this has been the only, or even the main, influence on them.

7

HONOR AND THE LAW

In Europe (and in the New World) notions of honor have since the Renaissance generally operated largely outside the normal legal system. "Why do you mention Law between Gentlemen?" asks a character in one of Fielding's novels, "A Man of Honour wears his Law by his Side."[1] Montaigne already observed that "there are two sets of laws, those of honor and those of justice, in many matters quite opposed."[2] This was especially evident where honor, though an important value among the elite, was virtually unrecognized by the law (as, for instance, in eighteenth-century England or in the antebellum South). Yet it was hardly less true in countries such as Spain and Germany, where honor has long been recognized and protected by the law. Even in those countries honor was mainly important outside the official law, and often enough the honor code was inconsistent with the law of the state.

The inconsistency was of various kinds. The honor code might call for the punctilious fulfillment of obligations that the state refused to enforce, notably gambling debts. Alternatively, it might impose obligations unknown to the courts; thus, in Fielding's *Jonathan Wild*, Mr. Snap holds the Count la Ruse under arrest in his (Mr. Snap's) home for debt, as, under the law, he is entitled to do. The author remarks that "tho' Mr. Snap would not (as perhaps by the nice Rules of Honour he was obliged) discharge the Count on his Parole; yet did he not (as by the strict Rules of Law he was enabled) confine him to his Chamber" but instead allowed him the "Liberty of the whole House."[3] The code of honor might lead a man to challenge another to a duel for an offense that the state viewed as being too trivial to merit attention: we know, for instance, of an officer in the Austro-Hungarian army who was jostled by a lady in a crowd and ended by calling out the man who accompanied her.[4] The code might insist on satisfaction for offenses

1. Fielding 1983, 364 (*Amelia*, book 9, chapter 3).
2. Montaigne 1958, 85 (book 1, chapter 23).
3. Fielding 1932, 21. The episode is to be found at the beginning of book 1, chapter 4.
4. Mader 1983, 46.

that were entirely outside the purview of criminal law; in the late nineteenth century, for example, it was not in Germany a criminal offense to seduce a man's unmarried daughter if she was over sixteen years of age; but this was a classic occasion for a duel. And even when the law did offer a remedy, honor might demand that a man reject it in favor of self-help. This too was already noted by Montaigne: "He who appeals to the laws to get satisfaction for an offense to his honor, dishonors himself."[5] In Germany at the end of the nineteenth century, for instance, a deceived husband could, if he was divorcing his wife for adultery, also demand that either she or her lover or both be prosecuted for the offense in the criminal courts.[6] But if the parties involved belonged to the upper classes, there would be no question of a criminal prosecution, only the possibility of a duel—itself of course illegal.[7] Indeed, the most glaring inconsistency between law and honor in Europe lay in the fact that the honor code insisted on the use of a violence that the law frequently condemned. Pitt-Rivers goes so far as to say that "the conflict between honour and legality is a fundamental one which persists to this day."[8]

Yet personal honor is a right very similar to a legal right. Montaigne sees the laws of honor as being opposed to the laws of justice; but he calls both "laws" (*loix*). Where there is personal honor there are therefore often courts of honor, even when the law they administer is op-

5. Montaigne 1958, 85 (book 1, chapter 23). Pitt-Rivers (1977, 9) writes, "To go to law for redress is to confess publicly that you have been wronged and the demonstration of your vulnerability places your honour in jeopardy, a jeopardy from which the 'satisfaction' of legal compensation at the hands of a secular authority hardly redeems it." This is misleading. To challenge your opponent to a duel is also normally to confess publicly that you have been wronged; in such cases the law is rejected not because it entails publicity, but because it does not offer the offended party the opportunities that the duel does: to prove, by his readiness to risk his life, that he is a man of honor, and personally to inflict physical damage on his opponent. Pitt-Rivers' argument only applies in very particular cases, notably, the secret revenges of Spanish drama.

6. Under § 172 of the German penal code, adultery carried a maximum penalty of six months in jail. (This article was removed from the code only in 1969.)

7. Moreover, as von Liszt (1908, 390 n. 3) maliciously pointed out, an adulterer who killed the deceived husband in a duel thereby rendered himself immune from prosecution for adultery. The reason is that the husband, being dead, could not initiate the proceedings for a divorce that were a necessary condition of such a prosecution.

8. Pitt-Rivers 1977, 9. Yet Lévy, Muxel, and Percheron (1991, 109–10) found that 84 percent of those they sampled associated honor with respect for the law, and only 16 percent associated it with the idea of outside the law.

posed to the law of the state. This was the case, for instance, of the *Ehrenrat* of the Austro-Hungarian army. The duel was officially illegal, not only under civil law, but even under military law; yet officers were frequently forced to leave the army if they refused to fight a duel in circumstances where the *Ehrenrat* thought that it was incumbent upon them to do so.[9] The contrast between the law administered by a court of honor and the ordinary law of the land was not always as harsh as this. For instance, the English Court of Chivalry, when it functioned as a court of honor in the seventeenth century, was opposed to the common law in the sense that it "gave remedy for words not actionable at law, tending to the dishonour of knighthood, or of anybody bearing arms";[10] but at the same time, by offering remedies of this kind, it clearly tended to discourage dueling.

In sum, honor is a notion that from a formal point of view fits easily enough into a legal system, but that in modern Europe, above all because of its links with the duel and other forms of violence, has had a generally uneasy relationship with the main body of the law.

The situation among the Bedouin[11] is very different. Honor (*'ird*) plays a major role—in fact several major roles—in the main body of Bedouin law; and there are almost no rights or duties connected with *'ird* that function outside the law. This places the student of Bedouin honor in a privileged position. The English word 'honor', like its equivalents in the other major modern European languages, has a huge range of meanings. The Bedouin word *'ird*, in contrast, is used only in a limited number of contexts, and the notion of *'ird* has the sharpness of outline that is characteristic of Bedouin legal concepts in general.[12]

The Bedouin in Sinai are notable for their legalistic mentality, and they share with their neighbors to the east a system of customary law that is remarkable for its sophistication, and is a central feature of the culture. In each tribe there are a number of men who are generally

9. Mader 1983, 100, 117–18. Contrast the case of Captain Beilby, in chapter 3 above. Mader, incidentally, offers a good survey of military courts of honor in other German-speaking states, e.g., Prussia and Bavaria.

10. Squibb 1959, 101, quoting a pleading from the year 1700.

11. Unless the context clearly indicates otherwise, the term 'Bedouin' refers to the Bedouin of the Sinai Peninsula and those of their neighbors who share the same legal system. Stewart 1987b gives a brief account of the main regional types of Bedouin law.

12. For a recent account of Bedouin honor, see Kressel 1992b, reprinted with minor revisions in Kressel 1992a, 195–216.

recognized as judges. Disputes are brought before them by consent of the parties concerned. The procedure is adversarial and, in its essentials, of a kind familiar to us: there is a plaintiff and a defendant, a clearly defined legal issue which is set out in the pleadings of the parties, and a judgment. If either party objects to the judgment, he[13] can initiate proceedings which in substance (though not in form) amount to an appeal.

The Bedouin have different types of judge for different types of dispute: one sort for blood disputes, another for disputes about land, another for jurisdictional disputes, and so on. There is also one special type of judge known as the Manshad,[14] and any dispute relating to *'ird* will come before the Manshad. The plaintiff in such a dispute claims that the defendant has wrongfully dishonored him, and seeks to be made whole by means of an award (which is also called a "manshad"). The award will generally consist both of money and of certain symbolic elements (on which see below).

There are two ways in which one may impugn a man's *'ird*. One is by what I shall call a *primary impugnment*. This can take a number of forms; a simple example is a sexual offense against a woman. Every Bedouin woman, whether married or not, is from a legal point of view the responsibility of her guardian (*walīy*),[15] that is, her closest adult male agnate (father, brother, father's brother, or whomever). A man who enters into a sexual relationship with a woman not his wife thereby offends against her guardian's *'ird* and renders himself liable to give a manshad to the guardian.

The defining characteristic of the primary impugnment is that the act itself is what besmirches the victim's *'ird:* he is being treated with disrespect. Normally, this is no part of the transgressor's intention: in the above example, for instance, we may assume that the offender is interested only in the woman, and has nothing against her guardian.

The other way in which A may impugn B's *'ird* is by *blackening* him.[16] A will say, "May God blacken B's face," or words to that effect. A may also set up a black flag, or a black stone, in some appropriate place,

---

13. In the Bedouin law of this area women have virtually no legal personality; in particular, they cannot sue or be sued. In this, as in many other respects, Bedouin law contradicts Islamic law. See further Stewart 1991.
14. Stewart 1988–90, 2:253, s.v. *manšad.*
15. Stewart 1988–90, 2:279.
16. Stewart 1988–90, 1: index, s.v. "blackening"; 2:263.

for example, near a well, where people will see it and ask who put it there and why.[17] A blackening is like an accusation that the man impugned *has already done* something that dishonors him: his right to respect is being denied.

The list of actions that dishonor a man—the ones, that is, that justify his being blackened—is short and fairly generally agreed on. Incomparably the most important in practice is failure to meet the obligations that one takes upon oneself as a guarantor.[18] It is not in general dishonorable for a man to have illegitimate sexual relations with a woman, but it becomes so when a special relationship of trust has been established, for example, when the man is accompanying the woman on a journey, or when the two reside in the same encampment. It is dishonorable to attack one's companion on a journey, or to abandon such companions in a fight. Robbery is not dishonorable, but theft carried out behind the victim's back (e.g., from a cache of grain) is. It is dishonorable to embezzle a deposit held in trust (*amāna*).[19] A classic honor offense arises from the institution of curatorship. Let us say that a friend of mine dies after nominating me as the curator (*wadīʿ*) of his infant sons. It is now my duty to look after their legal interests, e.g., to represent them in any legal action that may arise in relation to their property. If instead of doing this I take advantage of my position to, say, convert the property to my own use, then my wards will have the right to blacken me.

Bedouin *ʿird* is reflexive: if I do not respond properly to my *ʿird* having been impugned—whether in a primary way or by a blackening—then my *ʿird* is lost. If my wards (now grown to a man's estate) blacken me, there are only two ways I which I can retrieve my *ʿird*. One is to surrender and give them the property that they claim is rightfully theirs. The other is to fight by suing them before the Manshad. I may allege, for instance, that their inheritance was depleted not by my dishonesty, but by six successive years of drought. If the judge is not convinced, then I shall have to meet my wards' claim, but at least my *ʿird* will thereby be restored. If I win the case, that is, if I am awarded a manshad, then my *ʿird* will also be made whole again. The symbolic elements in a manshad—whether for a primary offense or for a wrongful blackening—are the counterpart of the symbolic elements

17. See Dresch 1987 for further references to this practice in Arab customary law.
18. See further the part of chapter 8 below that deals with the guarantee.
19. Stewart 1988–90, 2:194.

in a blackening: my wards will be obliged to set up white flags at various places, for instance, one at the place where they blackened me, and three others at commonly frequented wells.[20]

In any society that is concerned about honor, the question will quite often arise as to whether a particular action constitutes an impugnment of honor, and if so, how serious an impugnment. Most of the dueling codes deal with this problem, if only briefly. By the late nineteenth century they generally distinguished three classes of offense, each of which had different consequences for the subsequent proceedings. The most serious type of offense was physical (e.g., the slap on the face), and below this there were two grades of insult, aggravated and simple.[21] But of course a categorization as elementary as this could be no more than a rough guide, especially since the codifiers disagreed among themselves about a number of important details; some, for example, counted a mere discourtesy (e.g., a failure to return a greeting) as a simple insult, whereas others did not count it as an insult at all (which meant that it was not necessary to respond to discourtesy with a challenge).

Such problems arise equally among the Bedouin. Given the complexities of the real world, it is not always clear whether a given action is an affront to a man's '*ird*; and if it is an affront, it will still have to be decided—either by a judge or by negotiation between the parties—what kind of a manshad is due. It may not even be certain whether a given act or deed is a blackening, since the form of a blackening is not exactly fixed. For instance, one man said to another, "You people leave your faces [i.e., your honor] with your womenfolk,"[22] and it had to be decided whether this was a blackening or merely an insult (in the event, it was judged to be a blackening). It seems that in such cases the judges decide according to how a reasonable man would understand a given action or sentence, rather than according to the intentions of the speaker.

20. For actual instances of flags being raised, see Stewart 1988–90, 1: index, s.v. "flags."

21. See Bryson 1938 (quoting an Italian authority of the late nineteenth century); Rivanera 1961, 189–204 (which includes extensive references, especially to the French literature); and Mader 1983, 45–47.

22. In Arabic, *intuw wjūhkuw bitxallūhin 'ind ḥrayyimkuw.* Women are associated with dishonor in various ways, one of them being in that they wear black clothes.

In a dispute a man will, of course, often be interested in representing his opponent's actions in the worst possible light; and since a blackening is more serious than a mere insult, there will be a tendency to argue that a given form of words constitutes a blackening rather than an insult. But this may be done in a moderate way,[23] and Bedouin do not in general feel the need to prove themselves by seeing insults where none is intended, or affronts to their 'ird where none exists.[24]

The Bedouin lived, until recent times, in a society without central authority. Each tribe had a leader (the sheikh), but he was no more than the representative of the tribe in its dealings with the outside world. In these circumstances, certain functions that in our own legal system are performed by the state, were (and are) among Bedouin performed by institutions of a quite different kind.

The mainspring of the whole machinery of law is what I shall call the blood-money group. This is a group of adult males—in central Sinai usually around ten, but in other areas often many more—who are mostly each other's closest agnates, and who act as a politico-legal unit: on the one hand they are committed to defending each other's interests in any dispute, and on the other hand they share liability for each other's misdeeds. The Bedouin sum it up by saying "they pursue and they are pursued together."

The machinery powered by the mainspring is very elaborate, and a large part of it involves the notion of 'ird. In the next chapter I shall show how 'ird is employed in the structure of legal institutions that serve a remarkable variety of purposes.

23. For instance, the man against whom the very gross expression recorded at the top of Stewart 1988–90, 1:3 was directed did not insist that it be treated as a blackening (though he could have). Instead, he was willing to have it tried as an ordinary insult (Stewart 1988–90, Text 4, gives the judgment in this case).

24. Contrast, for instance, the remarks about the Sarakatsani quoted in chapter 5 above.

8

How to Do Things with Honor

The Home

One day in January 1978 a young Bedouin man, whom I shall call Faraj, was feeling ill. An epidemic of head colds had been sweeping the tribe, and he had probably caught one. He and his wife 'Yēdih were at the time camped with two other families in one of the most beautiful wadis of central Sinai. Its high walls provided protection from the cold winds of winter, and allowed the families to live in the open air without having to put up their tents. Early that morning most of the inhabitants of the camp had gone about their business: the men had taken the camels to the well to bring back water, and the women and children had driven the goats to pasture. Only the young couple remained.[1]

Now 'Yēdih was also feeling unwell. She and Faraj had scarcely ceased quarreling since their marriage some three years earlier, and when Faraj told 'Yēdih to do some job—according to one account he asked her to make a cup of tea,[2] according to another he ordered her to take their camel to graze[3]—she decided that she had had enough. Picking up her infant daughter, she went to the home of their neighbor Salāmih, a few score meters away in the wadi.

This was a standard move; a Bedouin woman who quarrels with her husband can always take refuge with the head of some other family. The man in whose home she takes refuge will then act as a mediator between her and her husband. After a day or two the husband usually admits he was in the wrong and pays his wife a small sum by way of amends. She then returns to her own home.

But in this particular case it was otherwise. Faraj, losing his temper completely, followed her into Salāmih's home. (Since the people were living in the open air, the home was simply the area around the

---

1. I myself was also in the camp, but not in sight of 'Yēdih and her husband. Only late in the day did I learn of what had transpired between them.
2. Stewart 1988–90, 1:15.
3. Stewart 1988–90, 1:12.

hearth.) There he hit her a couple of times with a stick, after which she returned to her own home.[4] Faraj had now committed offenses against two people. One was his wife's father (her guardian). Here the offense consisted in beating her in circumstances where he was forbidden to do so (he would have been within his rights to hit her in the same way in their own home or outside any home). The other victim was Salāmih, and the offense consisted in violating the peace of Salāmih's home; when the case came to court Salāmih claimed an award for Faraj's having entered the home without permission, an award for his having beaten 'Yēdih there, and an award for his having removed her from the home by force.[5] The fact that Salāmih and his family happened to be absent when the violation occurred was, from a legal point of view, entirely irrelevant.

When 'Yēdih took refuge in Salāmih's home, she placed him under the obligation to protect her. Through no fault of his own he had failed to do so. This created a new obligation, which was, of course, like his original one, not to 'Yēdih, but to her father. It was now Salāmih's duty to take whatever steps might be necessary to ensure that 'Yēdih's father received the blood money due to him for the beating. In this particular case the matter was simple, since Faraj made no difficulties about appearing in court. All that Salāmih had to do was to represent 'Yēdih's father in the proceedings (Salāmih being a far better lawyer than 'Yēdih's father); and Faraj was condemned first to pay the blood money, and then the award to Salāmih himself.[6] But if Faraj had somehow evaded payment of the blood money, it would have been Salāmih's duty to pay it to 'Yēdih's father.

Salāmih's obligation to 'Yēdih's father was one of honor; that is to say, if Salāmih had failed to do what he was supposed to do, then 'Yēdih's father would have had the right to blacken him. Faraj's action had placed Salāmih's 'ird at stake. The triangular structure established in this case is characteristic of Bedouin law, and appears in several quite different contexts. It is represented in figure 1 (see p. 98 below),

---

4. It was a matter of dispute whether he actually dragged her back to their home (Stewart 1988–90, 1:24), but it was clear in any event that she acted under constraint.

5. Stewart 1988–90, 1:24.

6. Stewart 1988–90, 1:11–12. The proceedings were quite protracted despite the fact that Faraj offered no defense; the original judgment did not give 'Yēdih's father all that Salāmih felt was his due, and so Salāmih appealed it.

Salāmih being the master of the home, Faraj the peace offender, and 'Yēdih's father the peace victim.

The protection of the master of a home extends to all those who are legitimately within it. It is not uncommon for women to seek refuge from their husbands, but of course normally those in the home are either members of the household or their guests. There was a case in the mid-1980s in which one man stabbed another in the home of a third, the perpetrator rushing in upon the victim from outside the home. The victim's host, though in no sense to blame for the event, properly accepted liability; since the perpetrator could not easily be brought to pay blood money, the master of the home paid it out of his own pocket. He expected eventually to be able to recover the sum from the perpetrator.

This was an unusually violent case. It does however happen from time to time that one guest insults, or even hits, another,[7] and when this occurs precisely the same triangular structure is created. The host must see to it, one way or another, that the injured guest is made whole; and if the host fails in this duty, the injured guest has the right to blacken him.

The notion that the home offers some special protection is, of course, firmly embedded in our own legal system, and has its roots far back in the Middle Ages.[8] The old Germans talked of *Hausehre*, 'house honor'.[9] We mostly think of the protection in the context of the members of the household being safe from intruders. This was equally true in the remote past. To kill or injure a man in his own home was often treated as a more serious wrong than to do so elsewhere.[10] A common feature of medieval German laws is that a killer is safe from private vengeance as long as he is in his own home.[11] A home also enjoyed various kinds of protection against searches by the authorities,[12] and a

7. The texts in Stewart 1988–90, 1:1–10 deal with such a case.

8. For Germany, the standard work is still Osenbrüggen 1857 (which concentrates on the twelfth to the sixteenth century); for Spain see Orlandis 1944, while for Italy there is an admirable study by Salvioli (1892). Trabandt 1970 is a brief survey that covers a considerable part of Western law on the subject, from the Romans to the present. Amelung 1986 discusses current German law, but also uses the anthropological and psychological literature.

9. *Deutsches Rechtswörterbuch*, s.v. *Hausehre*.

10. Trabandt 1970, 60–85, 91–92 gives examples from Germanic law.

11. Osenbrüggen 1857, 24.

12. Osenbrüggen 1857, 29–32.

man might even have some degree of immunity from arrest while he remained in his own house.[13] The old Austrian laws, which are particularly explicit, deal at length with such offenses as forcefully entering a home, breaking its doors or windows, and throwing missiles into the home. It is often even forbidden to stand outside the house and demand that one of its inhabitants leave it. Insults or other hostile actions are punished with particular severity if they are directed against a member of the household inside the home.[14]

I never heard of any case among the Bedouin of someone being harmed in their own home by an outsider, nor do I recollect the possibility being raised in discussion. But it could of course happen, and the way the law would deal with it is clear: if, let us say, the master of the home were himself the victim, then he would receive amends under two distinct headings, one as the victim of the insult or injury, the other as the master of the home.

The European laws also accept that a guest in a home enjoys some protection, though less than does a member of the household. In Germany in the later Middle Ages the guest was, broadly speaking, protected against his enemies, but not against the authorities.[15] I have not noticed a clear account of what happened in Germany when an offense was committed by a third party against a guest while he was in the host's home, but it sounds as if this may have been viewed (as it is among the Bedouin) as constituting an offense against the guest and a separate offense against the host.[16] This idea is still not extinct: "'You jist insulted me [. . .] You jist used violence in my house on one a my guests,'" says a character in a popular novel.[17] For Italy I did come across a clear analysis of the case of the insulted guest. It appears in the work of one of the Italian honor theorists, Giovanni Possevino (1520–49). His words deserve to be quoted at length:

> To give the lie in the home of another is to injure two people at the same time: [there follow some remarks about the injury done to the victim.] And that to give the lie to one in the home of another is to show contempt for the master of the home may be seen from the fact that he who has gone to the home of another assumes in going there

13. Osenbrüggen 1857, 25.
14. Osenbrüggen 1857, 57–60.
15. Osenbrüggen 1857, 47–48.
16. See Osenbrüggen 1857, 63, 66 (the Augsburg law), 71.
17. Wambaugh 1986, 198.

that he will be safe there, for otherwise he would not go, and he goes there implicitly under the faith [*fede*] of the master of the home. Whence, if the guest is dishonored in this home, it is as if the host's faith were broken; whence, he who gives the lie, who has in a certain sense caused the master of the home to fail to keep his faith, thereby insults him [*lo uiene ad ingiuriare*], and in insulting him shows that he does not fear him, for if he feared him, he would hold him in respect, and not holding him in respect, he shows contempt for him. Thus he who gives the lie or in some other way offends in the home of another shows disdain for the master of the home, unless it is to be assumed that the master consents to the insult; and thus that he allows him who has trusted him to be insulted; for it is not to be presumed that a gentleman does not have to show respect for another [*& cosi che lasci fare ingiuria à colui che si fidaua di lui, perche non si presume, che uno gentilhuomo non habbia à portar rispetto all'altro*]. [. . .]

[Question:] If both the master of the home and the man to whom the lie was given are insulted and offended against, as you say, at the same time: which one of them must resent it [*risentirsi*] most, and first?[18]

[Answer:] I think it is the master of the home who must resent it most and first, both because he may be suspected of the treachery of having broken faith [*per lo sospetto del tradimento d'hauer rotta la fede*], and for other reasons. The man to whom the lie was given is less insulted [. . .][19]

Possevino considers that both the injured parties should challenge the offender, first the host, and then the man to whom the lie was given (or

---

18. The verb *risentirsi* is evidently used here to mean not only that the subject feels resentment but also that he challenges the one who has insulted him. I would guess that the rare and obsolete reflexive use of 'resent' in English ('he resented himself' and the like) that is noted in the *Oxford English Dictionary* (s.v. "resent," v. section 5.b) comes from the Italian. More commonly, the English simply used 'resent' as a transitive verb in this sense: see Fielding 1932, 55, 57 (*Jonathan Wild*, book 1, chapter 13); and for a corresponding use of the noun 'resentment', see Fielding 1983, 364 (*Amelia*, book 9, chapter 3). These usages are not recorded in the *Oxford English Dictionary*.

19. Possevino 1553, 297. I consulted the copy of this work that is in the rare book collection of the Van Pelt Library, University of Pennsylvania. In this copy the pages in this part of the book are in the correct order, but they are not correctly numbered. There are two different pages that carry the number 297, and the passage quoted comes from the first of them.

who was otherwise offended).[20] The notion, so central to the Bedouin, of the host having an obligation to protect his guest, is not mentioned in these European sources;[21] nor, a fortiori, is the principle that if the guest suffers a wrong, then it is the host's duty to ensure that he receives amends.[22] Such ideas may well have existed, but if so, they were apparently not of much importance. Where the Bedouin have a tripartite structure, the Europeans have a bipartite one, or, in the case of offenses against guests, two bipartite ones: guest versus offender and host versus offender.

The reasons for the difference between the Bedouin and the Europeans on this score are no doubt multifarious. A European house was physically a very different structure from a Bedouin home, and European society offered the guest various forms of protection that did not exist among the Bedouin. A fuller examination of this question (using comparative material from other parts of the world) might well be illuminating.

THE GUARANTEE

Among the Bedouin the usual method of giving legal force to an agreement is to have it guaranteed.[23] When I sue D, for example, I want to be sure that he will actually appear in court on the day that we fix, and that if he loses the case, he will pay me whatever award the judge decrees. To set my mind at rest, D (the obligor) gives me (the obligee) G as a guarantor (*kafil*)[24] that D will indeed do these things. The guarantee takes the form of a pledge of honor: G places his *'ird*—often referred to in this context as his face (*wajh*)—in my hands. If D does not do what he was supposed to do, then it is G's duty either to induce D to do it, or, failing that, to give me satisfaction (e.g., by compensating me). If G does not carry out his duty to me, then I have the right to blacken G's face.

---

20. See further Bryson 1938, 6.

21. If Possevino only had verbal insults in mind, then this notion is, of course, scarcely relevant.

22. Some examples of ideas of this sort in various societies are to be found in Westermarck 1912–17, 1:577–78.

23. For other instances of three-party contracts of this kind in archaic legal systems, see Plucknett 1956, 629–30.

24. Stewart 1988–90, 2:241.

G will often be an elder, that is, a leader, of D's blood-money group. On the one hand, this is the reason why he is willing to act as guarantor for D: it is by doing just this kind of thing that he became a leader. On the other hand, this is why I accept him as a guarantor: he is a man with a long-standing reputation, and he is in an excellent position, if it should be necessary, to exert pressure on D: for D depends on his blood-money group to assure the safety of himself, his dependents, and his property in an anarchic world.

Almost every legal transaction among the Bedouin, be it the settlement of an intertribal border dispute,[25] an agreement about the payment and receipt of blood money,[26] or a divorce, involves the guarantee.[27] A man's guarantee is in effect backed up by his whole blood-money group: in the unlikely event that I blacken G and he fails to respond, I have the right to go on to blacken any other member of G's group. Given the importance that the Bedouin normally attach to their 'ird, I will quickly find someone who does respond, either by giving me (more or less) what is due to me, or by suing me before the Manshad.

As is evident from figure 1, the guarantee establishes a triangular structure similar to the one discussed in the preceding section. There are some important differences of detail between the two triangles as regards both the primary and the secondary offense, but they need not concern us here.

The pledge of honor was, of course, well known in medieval Europe. The basic idea there was the same as it is among the Bedouin: the obligee held the pledger's honor in his hands, as if it were a physical object, and if the pledger failed in his duty, then the obligee had the right to destroy that honor.[28] In Europe this was done by a variety of means; for example, in the later Middle Ages and in early modern times the obligee commonly had the right to spread abroad written

25. Stewart 1986, 9; Stewart 1988–90, 1:191.

26. For instance, Stewart 1988–90, 1:32–33.

27. Stewart 1988–90, 1: index, s.v. "guarantee," offers many more examples.

28. The European pledge of honor has not yet been studied in depth, but various brief accounts exist. Brückner 1971– and Mohrmann 1971– both give further references. The pledge of honor was closely connected with the pledge of (Christian) faith and the pledge of (feudal) fealty (see, e.g., Siegel 1894, 12–13, 15); these institutions are also not well understood. For a fuller account of the Bedouin guarantee, see Stewart 1990 (which includes a comparison with certain features of Germanic law).

texts denouncing the defaulting pledger and pictures in which he was represented in a degrading fashion. I am not aware that this particular practice existed in England, but the pledge of honor certainly did, and in seventeenth-century drama we still find phrases like "pawning our honours then to meet again" (1625) and "my honour's pawn'd for it" (1627),[29] while the expression 'to engage one's honor', where 'to engage' means "to deposit or make over as a pledge,"[30] is very common indeed.[31] Another familiar phrase, 'to redeem one's honor',[32] belongs to the same group. At least as late as the mid–eighteenth century the nature of the transaction involved seems to have been well understood;[33] the relevant phrases, in other words, had not yet become idioms whose literal meaning had been forgotten (as happened, say, to 'pledging one's troth').

If the pledge of honor were known only from medieval Europe, or only from among the Bedouin, one might be tempted to dismiss it as something marginal and idiosyncratic. But the fact that it is found in two such disparate cultures shows that it must be taken seriously, and that any theory of honor must be able to accommodate it. Consider again Pitt-Rivers' well-known characterization of honor: "a sentiment, a manifestation of this sentiment in conduct, and the evaluation of this conduct by others."[34] None of these three items lends itself easily to being viewed as a pledge. Liepmann's basic notion of honor as "the possession of certain qualities, specifically those qualities that determine a person's worth"[35] is equally problematic in this context, as is also his subjectified honor (the feeling of self-worth).

One might, however, be tempted to think that a man's reputation

29. Barber 1957, 166, 169, and cf. 190.

30. *Oxford English Dictionary*, s.v. "engage," v., section I. To this day one says in French *engager sa parole (d'honneur)* 'to pledge one's word (of honor)'; and the phrase *engagement d'honneur* means a promise or an oath.

31. For instance, Barber 1957, 177, 178, 183, 188, 190.

32. Barber 1957, 181, 191.

33. In book 1, chapter 6, of *Jonathan Wild*, the need arises to bribe a serving maid in order that she may aid the Count la Ruse in escaping from Mr. Snap's home. Wild tells the girl that "besides his [i.e., the count's] Promises, which she might depend upon being performed, she would receive from him [i.e., the count] twenty Shillings and Ninepence in ready Money, [. . .] and that besides his Honour, the Count should leave a Pair of Gold Buttons (which afterwards turned out to be Brass) of great Value in her Hands as a farther Pawn" (Fielding 1932, 32).

34. Pitt-Rivers 1968, 503.

35. Liepmann 1909, 12. Cf. chapter 2 above, n. 23.

(Liepmann's "objectified honor," Schopenhauer's "honor, taken objectively") could function as a pledge. This is how Barber usually understands phrases like 'to engage one's honor',[36] and we do, after all, say things like "I'd stake my reputation on it." But a moment's thought will show that we are then referring to an act that is in fact impossible. A distinguished epigrapher, for instance, cannot actually stake her reputation by saying, "This inscription comes from Asia Minor, and dates from the fifth century. I hereby stake my reputation on it." Later, when it turns out that the inscription comes from Syria and dates from the second century, the reputation of the epigrapher, even if her statement becomes known, may remain much what it was before.[37] One cannot stake one's reputation because one does not have sufficient power over it; and for the same reason one cannot pledge it.

Another phrase may also seem relevant here. I may say, for instance, "My reputation rests in your hands." This is reminiscent of the way the Bedouin talk of holding or grasping the guarantor's 'face'.[38] Now my reputation is other people's good opinion of me. It may rest in your hands in the sense that you are in a position to destroy it: I might use the phrase when you know something about me which, if you were to spread it about, would greatly reduce me in the estimation of others. And there is no logical difficulty in imagining a situation in which I give you a contingent right to destroy my reputation; thus, I might arrange things so that under certain circumstances you would gain access to a document that contains damning information about me that you would then be free to make public. Can the pledge of honor be looked on as analogous to this? Can we say that in the pledge of honor I give the pledgee the contingent right to do something that will destroy my reputation?

The damning information, in this analysis, would be the fact that I have failed to keep my promise. Now it may be that until the pledgee blackens me (or disseminates defamatory texts and pictures) no one knows that I have failed to keep my promise. In this case it is indeed the

36. Barber 1957, 242 offers an exception.
37. This is not to deny, of course, that a person's reputation may in certain circumstances *be* at stake, i.e., stand or fall according to the outcome of some series of events.
38. See, for instance, Stewart 1988–90, vol. 2, Texts 20.14 and 69.111. It has been remarked that in Iraq "the tribal Arab [. . .] often makes an oath by his sharaf [honor], and acts almost as if it were something one could hold in one's hand" (Roosevelt 1988, 164).

act of blackening (or whatever) that destroys my reputation. But secrecy is not a *necessary* component of the pledge of honor, and it is just as likely that even before the blackening, people know that I have failed to keep my promise, so that my reputation has already suffered. In such a case, the pledgee, in blackening me, is not destroying my reputation.

It would seem, then, that it is impossible to produce a satisfactory account of the pledge of honor if we equate honor with reputation. In contrast, the notion that honor is a right fits the pledge of honor perfectly: I pledge my right, and if I fail in my obligation, I lose my right.[39] It is because I have lost this right that it is open to the pledgee to blacken me (or whatever).

The view of honor as a right also fits another significant feature of the pledge of honor: the fact that honor is treated as if it were an object: for it was characteristic of the Middle Ages to treat rights as if they were things.[40]

Obviously, most of the arguments that have been used here about the pledge of honor apply also to locutions like 'on my honor'. Barber was puzzled by phrases of this kind, and placed the vast majority of occurrences of them in a category of their own. He suggested that in the phrase 'on my honor' the word 'honor' may originally have meant the speaker's reputation;[41] but it seems more likely that the speaker is staking his right to respect.

PROTECTION

In about 1976 a small blood-money group among the Aḥaywāt—its only members were three brothers—found itself under severe pressure from a large blood-money group. The large group, which numbered some fifteen men, was claiming that the small group owed them four

39. In essentially the same way, the owner of the copyright in a song might pledge his rights in the song. On the practice of pledging rights of various kinds in both medieval and modern law, see Hübner 1930, 485 f. Compare also Riezler (1929, 770), who states that in modern law it is impossible to pledge one's honor, since honor is neither a thing (*Sache*) nor a right (*Recht*), and hence not an object (*Gegenstand*) that can be pledged. Despite this perceptive observation, I am not aware that it has hitherto been suggested that honor, as it appears in the pledge of honor, is in fact a right.

40. Simpson 1986, 47, 103–5. Alternatively, one may say that it was characteristic of the Middle Ages to treat a wide variety of rights other than rights in land in the same way as rights in land, cf. Heusler 1885–86, 1:329–58, and especially 336.

41. Barber 1957, 324–25.

camels; the claim arose from a complicated series of events that had occurred in the late 1950s, and it was being revived now because the old leader of the small group had recently died. He had been succeeded by his son ʿLiyyān, the oldest of the three brothers. ʿLiyyān, unlike his father, was entirely lacking in forensic ability. Since he could not make up for this by the number of his supporters (having only his two brothers), he decided that he must seek help. ʿLiyyān therefore went to the sheikh of the tribe, hung his kerchief round the sheikh's neck, and said, "I place myself under your protection" (*ana dāxil ʿalēk*).[42] It was largely a matter of chance that the man to whom ʿLiyyān turned held the office of sheikh; what mattered to ʿLiyyān was that this man was the head of a large, united blood-money group that included two of the best lawyers in the tribe, and that ʿLiyyān's own little group was closer agnatically to this man's group than to any other. ʿLiyyān had acted wisely: the sheikh agreed to help him, and, with the support of the sheikh's group, ʿLiyyān was eventually able to extricate himself from his difficulties.

Once a man is under another man's protection, any offense against the protectee constitutes also an offense against the protector, to be precise, an offense against the protector's honor. Thus, for example, it happened that someone blackened a protectee. Now to blacken a man is, as we have noted, formally to impugn that man's ʿ*ird*. If the blackening is wrongful, that is, if the man is not guilty of the dishonorable action alleged, then the victim has a right to a manshad from the blackener. In this particular instance the blackening was indeed wrongful, and the protector saw to it that the protectee received not one, but two, manshads.[43] Having done this, the protector was himself awarded a manshad by the court, since his protection had been violated.[44]

Protection of this kind, in which the weak turn to the strong for help, either with regard to a particular dispute, or without any such limitation, is a phenomenon found in many societies. What is perhaps peculiar to the Bedouin is the extension of this notion to very particular interests, or, as the Bedouin themselves view it, to particular objects. How this works can be illustrated by the following

42. The same phrase could be used by a woman seeking refuge from her husband.
43. It is possible that the protectee got two manshads, rather than the normal one, precisely because he was under protection at the time of the offense against him.
44. For details, see Stewart 1988–90, 1:76.

highly simplified account of certain events that occurred in 1977–79.[45]

Two parties, whom I shall refer to as Protectee and Violator, were in dispute about the ownership of a field. Protectee was in possession of the field and was cultivating it, but feared that Violator would assert his claim by destroying the crop. Protectee therefore placed his crop under the protection of a neutral party, an important man from another tribe called Farrāj. This was a standard move: if I fear, say, that because of a dispute between us you are likely to seize or damage my camel or my truck, I will be well advised to place the object under the protection of a third party. The effect of doing this will normally be to deter you from taking unilateral action. You will be forced either to do nothing, or to pursue your claim through the courts.

Now in this particular instance Violator was confident of the justice of his claim, but there were circumstances that made it difficult for him to bring it before a court. He and his men therefore went to the field, tore down the barbed wire that surrounded it, and allowed their camels to graze on the young crop. This action violated Farrāj's protection. When protection of an object is violated the protector has a single duty: to get the party that violated the protection to defend himself in court against the claim of the party that placed the object under protection. This is not always easily done, and so it proved in this case. It actually took Farrāj over a year to get Violator to agree to a trial. Farrāj's obligation to Protectee was, of course, one of honor, and as the months went by without any progress, Protectee began to lose his patience, and Farrāj was in serious danger of being blackened.

At the trial Protectee sued Violator for the damage done to his crop and his fencing. The matter turned on the question of who owned the land, and judgment was for Violator. This meant that Violator had been acting within his rights in destroying Protectee's crop. It also meant that liability for the violation of Farrāj's protection lay not with Violator, but with Protectee.[46] Farrāj's honor had been impugned by the destruction of the crop, and by bringing the parties to court Farrāj

45. The case is documented in Stewart 1988–90, 1:123–61; a full account of it will be published elsewhere.

46. In other words, in terms of figure 1 it turned out that the Violator of protection and the Protectee were the same man. Similarly, a man can act as his own guarantor, so that if he defaults the defaulting obligor and the guarantor are the same man.

had shown that the impugnment was wrongful. The first trial was immediately followed by a second one in which Farrāj sued Protectee and was awarded a manshad.[47] Of course, if Protectee had won in the first trial, then Farrāj would have been suing Violator in the second.

It will be evident that in cases of this kind the notion of honor has been used to produce something that resembles the temporary restraining order in our own legal system. Protection of objects can also be used in quite different contexts. There was one leading man in the tribe who made it a habit to place certain grazing land under his own protection in the early spring. His purpose was not to benefit personally, but simply to ensure that people did not use it prematurely. At the right moment he would remove his protection, and the land would be open to all. This was an unusual use of protection. But protection is a standard legal instrument in various contexts: it can be used, for instance, by spectators to a fight to prevent the men (or women) involved from inflicting further injury on each other, by a woman's close agnate to prevent her from marrying someone who is not a close agnate, and by the elders of a blood-money group to ensure that junior members of the group do not undertake legal obligations without the consent of the elders. The complex details of these institutions need not concern us here; what I want to emphasize is that the basic structure by which an object (often an abstract rather than a physical one) is placed under protection, as represented in figure 1, can be used by practitioners of the law to achieve a variety of very different purposes.

47. In fact because of certain special circumstances the judge actually gave Farrāj two manshads (Stewart 1988–90, 1:161).

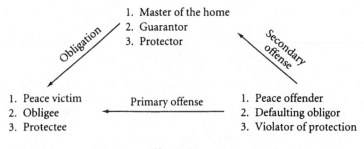

Figure 1

9

TYPES OF BEDOUIN HONOR

The two most prominent honor words among the Bedouin are *'ird* and *wajh*, 'face'.[1] Up to now I have concentrated on *'ird*, since anything that involves face also involves *'ird*, whereas the converse is not true; but the word 'face' is in fact far more commonly used. From more than one point of view, cases that come before the Manshad fall into two classes: sexual offenses and all the rest. A sexual offense is always an offense against the *'ird* of the woman's guardian, never against his face. All the other types of dispute—those relating to guarantees and to the various kinds of protection—involve activities in which the word 'face' is far more likely to be used than the word *'ird*. In some contexts the words 'face' and *'ird* can be used interchangeably; for example, one can give a guarantee by saying either "this in my *'ird*" or "this in my face."[2] In other contexts only the word 'face' can be used; for instance, there is a type of protection in which one is said to 'throw down faces',[3] and one could not talk of 'throwing down *'irds*'. Yet this type of protection also involves *'ird*, for to violate it is to 'cut the face' of the protector, and one who allows this to be done to him without getting a manshad from the offender loses his *'ird*.

'Face', unlike *'ird*, seems to be viewed as something of which a man cannot be stripped; but one can say that someone's face is worthless (*wijhih ma byanfa'*), or express the same idea in a more picturesque fashion. Thus one man says he won't accept the other's 'face', that is, his guarantee, and the other answers angrily, "Is my face perhaps treacherous?"[4]

The study presented here, insofar as it is ethnographic, has so far been of the lexical type; it has dealt with the place of *'ird* 'honor' and

---

1. *Wajh* (pronounced *wijh* by the Bedouin) means both 'face' in the literal sense and 'face' in the context of honor. For the sake of brevity, I shall, in what follows, simply write 'face', but this should always be understood to mean 'face in the context of honor'.
2. Stewart 1988–90, 2:199, 278.
3. Stewart 1988–90, 2:278.
4. Stewart 1988–90, 1:30; 2:34, Text 14.65.

wajh 'face' (when used in contexts connected with honor) in Bedouin life. One might also describe it as an institutional study, as dealing with the law relating to matters that may come before a Manshad. A conceptual study would have to cover a far wider range—just how wide is difficult to say, given the absence of a satisfactory definition of the notion of honor. But even if we confine ourselves to the law—if we ignore the possibility that people have extralegal rights to respect—there are various offenses against honor that are entirely unconnected with *'ird*. Insults, for example, are actionable: one man sued after the defendant had referred to him (not in his presence) as menstruating like a woman (the plaintiff had suffered badly from piles); another for the statement "You came to us barefoot from the Sa'īdiyyīn [a neighboring tribe], riding on a donkey, and I'm going to send you right back there." It is also an offense unreasonably to refuse hospitality.[5] I shall refer to these non-*'ird* offenses against honor as *affronts to dignity*.

The Bedouin themselves, however, do not categorize affronts to dignity as a separate group. One of the main ways in which disputes are grouped is according to the type of judge before whom they are heard. In addition to the various specialized types of judge (the Manshad, the judge for blood disputes, the judge for jurisdictional disputes, etc.) there is a residual category, known as the Elders of the Aḥaywāt,[6] who deal with all the various disputes that do not fall within the province of any specialized judge. Among many other things, the Elders deal with affronts to dignity.

In contrast to *'ird*, the honor involved in an affront to dignity is not reflexive. A man is as free to decide how to react to such an offense as he is to decide how to react to any other. This is not necessarily to say that he would be wise to ignore it. In one text, for instance, a man called Salāmih refers to another, Sālim, as a weakling because (in Salāmih's view) Sālim has been too ready to compromise and give way in various disputes.[7] If, like Sālim, you gain the reputation of being too quick to give way, then you may find that people begin to transgress against you in various ways because they believe that they can do so with impunity; but this need not affect your *'ird*. Sālim, for instance, was the elder of

5. Stewart 1988–90, 1:43–51 documents a case of this kind.

6. That is, among the Aḥaywāt tribe they are called the Elders of the Aḥaywāt. I presume that among the Sa'īdiyyīn tribe they are known as the Elders of the Sa'īdiyyīn, and so on.

7. Stewart 1988–90, 1:129–30.

his small group, and no one hesitated for a moment to accept his guarantee; nor could he—in contrast to a man who has no '*ird*—be rejected as a witness.

If we imagine horizontal honor among the Bedouin as being a pie, we can say that personal honor is a slice of that pie—a slice that, in contrast to the rest of the pie, has a special name, '*ird*. Among the Bedouin, personal honor is a relatively small part of the pie; in Europe it is larger, and it may be that in some instances (e.g., in medieval Iceland) it is the whole pie, that is, *any* failure by an equal to show proper respect is an offense against personal honor.

In Europe we can also find the pie being sliced according to principles unknown to the Bedouin. In a scene in Fielding's *Amelia*, Dr. Harrison, a cleric, makes a remark that Colonel Bath, a layman, sees as offensive. "'Sir, you are privileged,' says the Colonel, with great Dignity; 'and you have my Leave to say what you please. I respect your Order, and you cannot offend me.'" The colonel considers himself insulted (in the sense that he has not been treated with the respect that is his due), yet his personal honor is not threatened, since "the long-robed Gentry are exempted from the Laws of Honour"; the colonel says a little later, after another of Dr. Harrison's remarks to which he takes exception, "by all the Dignity of a Man, if any other Person had said the words you have just uttered, I would have made him eat them—Ay, d--n me, and my Sword into the Bargain."[8]

Now I think we may take it that each of the two men owes to the other the respect that one owes to an equal, and that Dr. Harrison has no right to insult the colonel. It follows then that the colonel's personal honor is more limited in scope than his horizontal honor. In the instances referred to in the paragraph before last the nature of the offense determines whether it is one against a man's personal honor or one against some other part of his horizontal honor; in this instance what determines how the offense is classified is not the nature of the offense but the status of the offender, and what is striking (and unknown among the Bedouin) is that two men may be equals and yet not belong to the same honor group.

In principle, the rights involved in affronts to dignity could take the place of '*ird* in the legal system. I could, for instance, say to you that I

8. Fielding 1983, 364–66 (book 9, chapter 3).

undertake to do such and such, and that if I don't do it, then you will have the right to insult me in any way that you wish. The idea of doing this has probably never crossed the mind of even a single Bedouin, but the implications of such an act are worth considering. It would differ from the pledge of honor in that it would be a purely bilateral transaction—it would not give a third party the right to insult me (whereas a man who is blackened loses his right to respect from the world).[9] But I could get round this by wholly renouncing my right to sue for affronts to dignity in the event that I fail to keep my undertaking. Even in this case, however, the effect of the pledge of honor would not be entirely achieved. In the pledge of honor what I stand to lose is my right to be treated as an upright man. In our imaginary example what I lose is much less than this, and I could not, for instance, be rejected as a witness.

The notion of honor is probably important in almost all Arab societies, but accounts that are both detailed and reliable are surprisingly few. I hope at a future date to analyze some of the material. For the moment, three brief observations.

The vocabulary of honor is much the same everywhere in the Arab world; but though words such as '*ird, sharaf* 'honor', '*ār* 'dishonor', and '*ayb* 'a shame, a disgrace' are very widely distributed, the meaning that is attached to them varies greatly from place to place. At least in some cases this may reflect substantial differences in ideas about honor.

Broadly speaking, the ideas about honor that I have described in this essay as being those of the Bedouin of central Sinai are also those of the Bedouin farther east, those of the Syrian Desert and Arabia. A similar structure of ideas exists also among many of the sedentary people who have come under strong Bedouin influence.[10]

9. In the same way, the European aristocrat who reneged on a pledge of honor was regarded as dishonorable (Rundstein 1905, 31–33 on Poland), and was no longer treated as an equal member of his group (Brauer 1930, 39–45 on Germany). Cf. also the verses of a defamatory text from the year 1523 issued by Hans von Besenrode (or Biesenrode) against Asche von Cram. In it the man being defamed is represented as saying "I Asche von Cram no longer belong in the order of knights / Since I have betrayed my honor to Hans von Besenrode" (Hupp 1930, 33).

10. See, for instance, Muhawi 1989, a useful account of honor in traditional Palestinian society.

Thanks to the admirable work of Bichr Farès (published in 1932), we can compare the ideas of the modern Bedouin with those of their pre-Islamic ancestors. The main difference between the two is perhaps this: that the ancient Bedouin used the word *'ird* in a much wider sense than do their descendants. Not only what the modern Bedouin view as actions that touch a man's *'ird* but also what I have called 'affronts to dignity' would in pre-Islamic times have been matters of *'ird*. The broad pre-Islamic notion of *'ird* was in fact much closer to the European notion of honor than is the narrow modern notion of *'ird*.

PART THREE

10

WOMEN

In societies where honor is important, it tends to be mainly something for men. In some societies women have no honor at all (as among many Bedouin tribes); in others their honor is of a limited or secondary nature. In part this is because women are so often excluded to a greater or lesser extent from public life. If there is vertical honor in such cases, then a woman's vertical honor is frequently no more than a reflection of that of her menfolk.[1] Where women do have personal honor, the main component of that honor is very often chastity; women are given little opportunity to display such virtues as courage in battle, and qualities of integrity that they display tend to be confined to the domestic sphere. If there is a system of reflexive honor, women are not normally direct participants in it: when a woman's honor is impugned and a counterattack has to be made, then it is usually a man who will make it. In the Icelandic sagas women are often represented as possessing a strong sense of honor, and where there is no alternative they themselves may take up weapons to revenge their honor;[2] yet even so, the way a saga expresses explicitly the fact that a woman has a strong sense of honor is by calling her a *drengr góðr*, a term that taken literally means 'a fine (young) man'.[3]

Honor is a notoriously paradoxical topic, and one of its most famous puzzles is the effect that women's behavior can have on men's honor. Don Lope, the central character of Calderón's drama *Secret Vengeance for Secret Insult*, suspects his wife. Soon he realizes from certain hints that his domestic troubles have become known to others. How can it be, he says in an anguished monologue, that when he has done everything that honor demands of him, shown courage in war, been courteous to the humble, generous to the poor, loved and respected his wife—how can it be that despite his impeccable conduct, he is

---

1. See, for instance, O'Leary 1987, 29; Jones 1959, 95; Martin 1984, 26, 128.
2. Gehl 1937, 34, 42, 57; Meulengracht Sørensen 1983, 21–22.
3. See appendix 2.

exposed to insult? What kind of court is it that condemns an innocent man?[4]

We have here a great division between two different kinds of dishonor, one brought about by a man's own misdeeds, the other by the misdeeds of others, usually women.[5] That the two should be united under a single concept may seem strange, yet it is characteristic of much of Europe and the Middle East that they are. It is sometimes suggested that southern Europeans are more affected by the chastity of their women than are northern ones, and there may be some truth in this. But the difference is probably largely one of degree. "No one was more dishonorable than a cuckold," writes an authority on medieval German honor,[6] and the thirteenth-century Arthurian romances from northern France suggest much the same.[7] As for the sixteenth and seventeenth century, "The idea that a woman's chastity or reputation for chastity affected the reputation of her menfolk is not peculiar to Spain; it occurs in many English plays."[8] The main difference in the dramatic treatment of the subject between the two countries seems to be that the notion of murdering the woman who is believed to be unchaste arises much less frequently on the stage in England than it does in Spain.[9] Some northern Europeans continued to be very concerned about sexual honor until quite recent times; for instance, in the decades before World War I many Germans considered that a man (of the appropriate class) would lose his honor if he should fail to challenge his wife's lover, or the seducer of his unmarried daughter, to a duel. In sharp contrast,

4. Calderón 1956, 3.229–55; Calderón 1961, 52. The last lines of the speech are "¿por qué [me] afrentas?, ¿por qué? / ¿En qué tribunal se ha visto / condenar al inocente?" Barber 1957, 275, remarks of cases of this kind in the English drama that "the man's conduct may have been quite beyond reproach, but he nevertheless loses honour."

5. Barber (1957, 141, 275) uses the term "reflected honor" to refer to the honor which one can lose solely through the behavior of others who are closely tied to one. In chapter 4 above the misbehavior of the ensign who was accused of drinking with the private soldiers is seen as reflecting on the honor of the entire battalion.

6. Jones 1959, 85.

7. Robreau 1981, 143–44.

8. Wilson 1953, 39. Barber gives numerous examples, and notes that references to this kind of honor in the drama become markedly more frequent in the second half of the seventeenth century (Barber 1957, 276).

9. Barber 1957, 275–76, 295. Barber is advisedly tentative about this; no one has yet made a quantitative analysis of Spanish drama of the kind that he produced for English drama.

the sexual mores of the upper classes in Italy seem already to have been quite relaxed in the seventeenth and eighteenth century: certainly nothing could be more alien to Wilhelmine Germany than an institution like the cicisbeo.

There are two different ways in which, without doing anything or having anything done to one, one's honor can be affected by someone close to one. One possibility is that someone close to one is treated in a dishonorable way. An example occurred among the Bedouin while I was in the field: a young man was alleged to have thrust his hand into the bosom of a young unmarried woman. There was no suggestion that she had offered him even the slightest encouragement. The girl's father received a substantial award from the Manshad. The judgment here would have seemed perfectly reasonable to the Romans: as Ulpian says, "a contumely (*iniuria*) affects us which is suffered by those who are subject to our power or are the objects of our affection."[10]

A second possibility is that someone close to one does something disgraceful. In the sphere of sexual honor there is an excellent example of this in a famous Egyptian story which has been the subject of a number of oral poems. An army sergeant called Mitwalli learns that his sister has become a prostitute. He tracks her down, kills her, chops up the corpse, and throws it from her balcony to the dogs. All this is described with unqualified approval by the authors of the poems, as is Mitwalli's subsequent exoneration in court.[11] What interests us here is that there is no hint of an attempt to find the man who first seduced the girl, or to take revenge on her customers (one of whom is a soldier in Mitwalli's unit): the whole emphasis is on the young woman herself.

It is characteristic of sexual honor that the two kinds of disgrace often come into play together. When a woman is seduced the usual reaction is both to see her as having been mistreated by the man and to view her as having done something disgraceful.

Don Lope's question can be turned on our model: how is it that he has lost his honor without having broken the rules of the honor code? One answer is that the model does not specify that it is only by break-

10. *Digest* 47.10.1.3.
11. Cachia 1989, 64, 269–322.

ing the rules of the code that one loses honor. Another answer is that his honor is not lost, it is merely moot.[12] He has been challenged, just as he would be challenged if he were given the lie; the code now tells him what he should do, and whether he retains his honor or loses it depends on his following its rules.

12. This notion is discussed more fully in chapter 11.

11

DISHONOR

The sources usually have a good deal to say about the honor code, but they are much less informative about the state of those who have lost their honor. Our own image of dishonor is perhaps formed from the upper classes of the nineteenth century: we think of the man who cheats at cards being expelled from his club, the woman whose sexual misconduct is notorious no longer being received in polite society. In the small world of the officers' mess, where expulsion as such was not possible, a man who was viewed as having acted dishonorably would be systematically shunned by all the other officers.[1] The regulations of a league of Franconian noblemen from the year 1517 include the rule that if one of their number is known to have acted in in a dishonorable fashion, then the others must not eat with him, nor drink with him, nor be his friend, nor keep company with him.[2] In essence, loss of honor means in these cases exclusion from the group. Just how seriously such exclusion can be taken may be seen from the same regulations: for they go on also to condemn to ostracism anyone who consorts with one who has been expelled.[3]

Dishonor of a kind imposed by law and not merely by society appears in the Swiss laws on the subject, which mostly date from the late medieval and early modern period. The man who has lost his honor cannot take an oath (i.e., testify), cannot take part in the Landsgemeinde (the assembly of the citizens of the canton), and cannot assume public office. All this is in essentials much like what we find among the Romans, except that here use is made of the word 'honor'. Furthermore, the Swiss forbade a man who had been dishonored to

1. British examples in Gilbert 1976, 80 (eighteenth century) and Douglas 1887, 21 (nineteenth century).
2. *Welicher under uns offentlichen wider Ere thet / also daß es kündig und offenbar were / mit dem oder denselben sollen wir andere nicht essen / trinken / eine Freundschafft oder Gemeinschafft haben.*
3. Lünig 1713, 4, quoted in Brauer 1930, 33. Cf. Brauer 1930, 45 n. 1, where other instances of this type of ostracism among organizations of German aristocrats are noted.

visit inns or any other places where honorable men gathered together.[4] Occasionally, even positive humiliation was employed. A visitor to Zug in 1731, after the town had suffered some political disturbances,[5] noted that in houses inhabited by certain of the citizens who had been held guilty of political offenses there were notices saying something like "This is the residence of the dishonorable Jakob Brandenberg," or whatever the man's name might be.[6]

As we saw in chapter 4, the Romans, though they did not have a word for honor, did distinguish between those citizens who were respectable and those who were not. The same is true of many other societies. The fact that a certain society has the notion of ignominy, dishonor, infamy, disgrace, or whatever does not entail that it also has the notion of personal honor (as defined here). What is more, I do not know whether there is anything that distinguishes the state of disgrace in societies that do have a concept of personal honor from the state of disgrace in those that do not. The material that follows is all—or almost all—drawn from societies that do have the concept of personal honor, but it may well be that similar material could be gathered from societies in which personal honor does not exist.

It was stipulated as part of the model of personal honor that the rules of the code are looked on as important. It seems to follow from this that the kind of respect that one has when one follows the code is important (as opposed, let us say, to the unimportant respect that one might enjoy by virtue of being a good bridge player). And from this it seems to follow further that the right that is lost when one is known to have failed to meet the standards of the code is also important. These inferences may be correct, yet it must at least be added that dishonor can affect its victim in rather subtle ways. This was so even in the Middle Ages, an era not always notable for delicacy of touch in such matters. In Chrétien de Troyes' version of the Arthurian romance *Erec and Enide,* Erec won and married Enide, and returned with her to his kingdom. They seemed set to live happily ever after,

4. On all this, see Osenbrüggen 1969, 111–38.
5. On which see Koch 1972, 104–6.
6. Osenbrüggen 1969, 131. The traveler says that the wording was something like "Hier wohnet der Ehr- und Wehrlose Jakob Brandenberg." On the formula *ehrlos und wehrlos,* see the section Honor and Violence in chapter 12 below.

But Erec was so in love with her that he cared no more for arms, nor did he go to tournaments. He no longer cared for tourneying; he wanted to enjoy his wife's company, and he made her his lady and his mistress. He turned all his attention to embracing and kissing her; he pursued no other delight. His companions were grieved by this and often lamented among themselves, saying that he loved her far too much. Often it was past noon before he rose from her side. This pleased him, whoever might be grieved by it [. . .] All the nobles said that it was a great shame and sorrow that a lord such as he once was no longer wished to bear arms.[7]

Erec had fallen into dishonor,[8] but as Chrétien says, "the matter was hidden from him," that is, he was not even aware of the fact, until one morning his wife revealed it to him. He then immediately took action to recover his honor.

Erec's situation perhaps resembles that of many deceived husbands. The husband is notoriously the last to know; and until he is enlightened, he is presumably in a state of dishonor without realizing it.[9] This also suggests that the manifestations of dishonor (to its subject) must in such a case be either nonexistent or at least very subtle.

The converse of Erec's case—where the subject views himself as being dishonored even though those around him do not—is also perfectly possible. The title of Kipling's story *His Private Honour* is a pun: the soldier is a private, and his honor is private, private in the sense that though he himself feels deeply disgraced by what has happened, it does not seem that this feeling is shared by those around him. It is true that one man in his company taunts him for having been struck without striking back, but that man is a Jew, a contemptible creature who epitomizes all that is weak and unmanly: this same Jew allows himself to be bullied unmercifully by the soldier in the period of frustration that fol-

7. Chrétien de Troyes 1991, 67 = 1987, lines 2396–424.
8. Chrétien does not explicitly say that Erec's *enor* is diminished, but the context makes it clear that this is so. Hartmann von Aue, in his German version of the romance, at this point states in so many words that Erec lost all his honor (Hartmann 1984, lines 2969–70). It must be added, however, that 'honor' very possibly does not refer to a right here, and that this example may well have to be counted as one that comes from a society that does not have the concept of personal honor.
9. In the speech from Calderón *Secret Vengeance for Secret Insult* that is discussed above, Don Lope remarks that the outrage he has suffered must indeed be widely known to have reached his own ears (Calderón 1956, 3.207–8; Calderón 1961, 52).

lows the blow. The other members of the company do not manifest any lack of respect for the soldier. The essence of the situation is that something has happened that is not covered by the ordinary rules: the soldier has been dishonored, but military discipline prevents him from taking any initiative to recover his honor. In these circumstances it is unlikely that the members of his company generally think any the worse of him.

There is a fine account of dishonor in Theodor Fontane's novel *Effi Briest* (first published in 1896).[10] Effi, the heroine, is a young woman from the minor aristocracy of Prussia. Shortly after her marriage she has a brief affair with a married man. This remains unknown to all but herself and her lover until nearly seven years later, when by sheer chance Effi's husband, Baron von Innstetten, discovers what has happened. He immediately resolves to challenge the lover, and writes a note to his (Innstetten's) friend and colleague Wüllersdorf, whom he wants to engage as his second. Wüllersdorf comes to see Innstetten, Innstetten tells Wüllersdorf the facts, and Wüllersdorf tries to dissuade him from the challenge. Innstetten explains, with obvious sincerity, that because of the passage of time he feels neither hatred nor even the urge for revenge towards the lover. Wüllersdorf then asks him why indeed he needs to fight a duel, and Innstetten replies, "with people all living together, something has evolved that now exists and we've become accustomed to judge everything, ourselves and others, according to its rules. And it's no good transgressing them, society will despise us and finally we will despise ourselves and not be able to bear it and blow our brains out."[11] Whether he likes it or not—and it is pretty clear that he does not like it—Innstetten's sense of honor is so strong that he believes that a failure to abide by the code would lead to the collapse of his self-respect (I take it that he sees the fact that society would despise him as no more that a contributory factor in achieving this effect). Innstetten next brings forth a quite different set of considerations:

> "I went to your place and wrote you a note and by doing that the
> game passed out of my hands. From that moment onwards, there

10. The novel is based on the events surrounding a real duel that was fought in 1886. Details can be found in any of the several annotated editions of the novel.

11. This quotation, like the one that follows, comes from the end of chapter 27. I have used the excellent translation by Douglas Parmée (Fontane 1967), changing it only to bring it a little closer to the original.

was someone else who knew something of my misfortune and, what is more important, of the stain on my honor; and as soon as we had exchanged our first words, there was someone else who knew all about it. And, because there is such a person, I can't go back."

"I'm still not sure," repeated Wüllersdorf. "I don't like using a stale cliché but there's no better way of putting it: 'I'll be as silent as the grave,' Innstetten."

"Yes, Wüllersdorf, that's what people always say. But there is no keeping a secret. And if you do as you say and are discretion itself towards others, even so *you* know about it [. . .] The fact of the matter is, that from this moment onwards I'm dependent on your sympathy (in itself not something very pleasant) and every word that you hear me exchange with my wife will be checked by you, whether you want to or not, and if my wife talks about fidelity or, as women do, sits in judgment on another woman, then I shan't know where to look. Or suppose it happens that, in some quite ordinary question of an affront having been given, I suggest that allowances might be made because there was no intention to insult, or some such thing, then a smile will cross your face or at least start to cross it and in your mind you'll be saying to yourself: 'Good old Innstetten, he has a real passion for running chemical analyses on insults in order to discover exactly how much insulting material they contain, and he *never* finds enough choking gas in them. He's never yet been choked by anything . . . ' Am I right, Wüllersdorf, or not?"

Wüllersdorf had risen to his feet. "I think it's terrible that you're right, but you *are* right. I won't torment you any longer with my question as to whether it's necessary. The world simply is as it is and things don't go the way that *we* want but the way that *others* want. All that pompous talk about 'God's judgment' is nonsense, of course,[12] we don't want any of that, yet our own cult of honor is idolatry. But we must submit to it, as long as the idol stands."

Here the world has been reduced to an absolute minimum, to a single man, a man who has himself advised Innstetten not to challenge the lover; yet Innstetten would rather fight, risking his life and allowing his domestic tragedy to become generally known, than have his friend know that he has violated the code of honor. Furthermore, there is no reason to believe that the world at large would take a radically different attitude from Wüllersdorf's: some might indeed think that Innstetten

12. The medieval idea that the outcome of a battle between two champions would reveal God's judgment as to a matter in dispute was apparently still being brought forward in some circles as a justification for dueling.

ought to challenge the lover, but there would clearly be no question of any overt sanction, such as expulsion from society, if it were to become known that he had failed to do so.

Innstetten is the spokesman of European honor in its last great efflorescence, and it might be thought that the refinement of feeling that he exhibits is unlikely to have existed in less sophisticated societies. I do not believe this to be the case. Innstetten is no doubt more articulate than men from earlier times, but he is not necessarily different from them. For the heroes, and indeed for the heroines,[13] of the Icelandic sagas dishonor sometimes seems to lie much more in what they feel about themselves than in anything that those around them manifest towards them, or perhaps even think about them.

Bedouin dishonor is also at the subtle end of the scale. When I asked an informant in a general way how people would treat a man who had submitted to being blackened, I was told that such a man would not be excluded from the company of other men, but that he would be treated as having no value (*gīmih*), that is, no attention would be paid to him, a rug would not be spread on the ground for him to sit on (as is usually done), and so on. In actuality, however, there was no man in the tribe who was treated in this way, nor did I ever hear of one (though the informant told me that he had seen one such case in each of two neighboring tribes). The same informant, having told me that so-and-so had been blackened and had not received a manshad, would in fact treat so-and-so with perfect politeness when he came to visit. Nor was he alone in such behavior. In a word, the social sanctions against a blackened man were, even in theory, rather feeble, and in practice (as far as I could tell) nonexistent.

To this must be added the rider that I knew of no man who was universally acknowledged to have submitted to being blackened. During the six years that I was in close contact with the Aḥaywāt, there was no clear case of a man submitting to being blackened, and I do not believe that there was any man in the tribe who would say of himself that he had done so: the alleged instances were apparently all surrounded by some doubt, arising, I suspect, from a certain halfheartedness in the blackener: for it is easy to blacken someone so publicly and

13. Gehl 1937, 34.

so clearly (and if necessary, so frequently) that there is no doubt at all about the matter.

The main consequence at law of having submitted to being blackened was that a man could be rejected as a 'paid witness' (*marḍawiy*).[14] I know of no case where this actually occurred, though I have no doubt that under the appropriate circumstances it might have happened. But incapacity to testify cannot among the Bedouin be considered a severe sanction, since if a man is asked to act as a paid witness it is normally precisely in a dispute in which he is neutral; and in all instances that I knew of, the paid witness renounced the fee that was due to him.

One might under these circumstances expect that many men would simply laugh at the possibility of being blackened. In fact precisely the opposite was the case. I believe that even the most disreputable men would have been disturbed by a blackening, and that most men would have gone to great lengths—if necessary, like Innstetten, endangering their lives—rather than submit to such a thing. The honor code was taken very seriously, and a guarantee, especially if it was from one of the leading men in the tribe, was as good as money in the bank. A failure to fulfill such an obligation would greatly reduce the influence and standing of such a man; but I think that in general—for the prominent and for the others alike—the most painful result of submitting to a blackening would have been the humiliation and the loss of self-respect.

One can, of course, lose one's '*ird* without being blackened, and there was one man—he appears in my work under the pseudonym 'Aṭiyyih—whom I knew who had clearly done so. He had been found guilty in a Bedouin court of having attempted to prostitute ones of his wives,[15] and it was well known that he sold the favors of one of his daughters (in the intervals between her various marriages). For these and other reasons—particularly the fact that he was a heavy drinker—'Aṭiyyih was certainly not much respected by most of his fellow tribesmen; yet even those who were most condemnatory of him did not treat him, as far as I could tell, any differently from the way that they would

14. Stewart 1988–90, 2:256. When the testimony of a witness is crucial to the decision of a case—and this is not true in most disputes—then the witness has a right to be paid for his testimony. Plaintiff and defendant make an equal payment, but the party that loses the case must reimburse the party that wins.
15. For some further details, see Stewart 1991, 121.

treat a man whom they recognized as being perfectly honorable, but whom they personally disliked; and there seemed to be a good many people who did not allow ʿAṭiyyih's disdain for the rules governing sexual honor to affect their relations with him. ʿAṭiyyih could no doubt be rejected as a paid witness, but this was not a matter of any real significance; and people continued to accept him as a guarantor.[16]

It will be obvious from the examples given above that we must distinguish carefully between the right to respect, the manifestation of respect to the person who receives it, and the feeling of respect. Each is logically independent of the other two, and it is easy to construct quite realistic situations in which one is present and the two others are absent, or two are present and the third is absent.

Erec, for example, lost the right to respect and the members of his court ceased to feel respect towards him; but they apparently continued to manifest respect to his face (he was, after all, a king). Innstetten, when he imagines the result of not challenging the lover, visualizes Wüllersdorf as having lost some of his feeling of respect for him, but he does not imagine Wüllersdorf as intentionally showing disrespect to him;[17] and what he imagines is compatible with Wüllersdorf's continued belief that Innstetten has a right to respect, that is to say, that he acted correctly in not challenging the lover. Sensible people who know Sir Walter Elliot do not feel much respect for him, but they acknowledge his right to respect and they manifest to him the degree of respect that is appropriate to a man of his standing.

There was a time, in the German lands, when a woman found guilty of adultery might be sentenced to have her hair cut off, or even to drag a dung cart through the streets.[18] By the late nineteenth century, measures of this kind had long fallen out of use, but after the duel and her separation from her husband, Effi Briest is excluded from society. Her very parents—who are by no means represented as unloving—refuse to allow her to live with them, since to do so would result in the extinction of their own social life. Society shows its disrespect for Effi in a way

---

16. Stewart 1988–90, 1:216.
17. Note, however, that the smile, or the beginning of a smile, that Innstetten mentions is an unconscious manifestation of disrespectful thoughts, and as such could well be taken as a manifestation of disrespect.
18. Dülmen 1990, 53.

that is less brutal, but scarcely less striking, than the methods of an earlier age. Yet it might appear that this kind of dishonor does not involve the loss of any right: after all, did Effi ever have a *right* to be invited to the homes of others, to be greeted by others, to have her invitations accepted by others?

The answer to this will appear if, for instance, we look at the beginning of Effi's marriage. Her husband was at the time the Landrat—that is, governor or administrator—of the (imaginary) district of Kessin in Pomerania. This senior position, to say nothing of his own social background, gave him a natural place in the small and close-knit aristocratic society of the area. Now if, after Innstetten brought Effi to Kessin, the members of this group had failed to invite her to their homes and had refused to accept her invitations, it would have been deeply insulting both to Effi and to her husband. Effi, as a respectable woman from an impeccable background, had every right (under the rules that applied in such circles) to be treated as a full member of the group; to behave to her otherwise would have been to tell her that she was unworthy just as clearly as if the statement had been made to her face. Effi's right to be treated as a full member of the group cannot necessarily be translated into a right to be invited by some particular family to some particular social occasion; but it does entail a right not to be insulted by being systematically excluded from the social life of the group.

The transition that a person makes from being honorable to being dishonorable may be marked in some formal fashion. A picturesque example was mentioned briefly in the discussion of the guarantee in chapter 8. In a large part of continental Europe—Germany, Poland, Bohemia and Moravia, and France—the dishonor of a man who defaulted after pledging his honor might be marked by the propagation of a defamatory text accompanied by an appropriate picture.[19] One

19. Künssberg 1925, 108 n. 272 = Künssberg 1965, 86 n. 272. The brief account of defamatory pictures in this work (Künssberg 1925, 106–12 = 1965, 46–50) is well worth reading. Defamatory pictures of this kind are known to have survived only from the German-speaking countries, and it seems to be uncertain whether the defamatory texts in the other countries mentioned were also sometimes accompanied by pictures. It was also often open to the obligee to defame the obligor purely verbally, and occasionally this was the only form permitted under the contract (Rundstein 1905, 29, referring to Poland).

such text was written in the year 1562 and directed against the mayor and council of Stolberg, a city in the Lower Harz mountains in central Germany. The picture that went with it may be described as follows.[20]

Three members of the council are riding backwards on a sow; the sow is eating a large turd. The councillors face to the left and each is chained by the neck to a gallows above them. On the back of each councillor is a raven. To the left of the picture, facing the sow's rear, a fourth councillor is depicted face down between the spokes of a wheel that lies horizontally at the upper end of a vertical pole; on top of the pole is yet another raven. This fourth councillor has his face turned to the other three. With his left hand he is holding up the pig's tail, and with his right hand he is pressing his signet under the tail. The councillor sitting farthest back on the sow is doing the same. The two councillors who are riding behind him are extending their signets in their left hands, as if to indicate that these signets too are to be treated in this fashion.[21]

Every element in the picture is, of course, heavy with symbolism, and many of its features occur again and again in such productions. To mention only a few points: riding backwards on a sow is a characteristically humiliating posture, and one that at this time was especially associated with Jews. The gallows signify execution by hanging, and the wheel signifies execution by breaking on the wheel.[22] Ravens were always to be found where the corpses of those executed were left. The signet signifies the pledge, and what two of the councillors are doing with their signets indicates how much value is to be attached to their word.[23]

20. A reproduction of the picture, together with a transcription of some of its accompanying text, is to be found in Hupp 1930, 66. Hupp's work is the only substantial collection of defamatory pictures and their accompanying texts. Kisch 1931 (reprinted in Kisch 1980) is a brief but important study of the subject; it offers a valuable account of the contents of Hupp's book, which is very rare.

21. This description is an expanded and slightly corrected version of one written in 1900 and reproduced in Künssberg 1925, 109 (= Künssberg 1965, 47–48). Künssberg 1925 reproduces several defamatory pictures; the 1965 edition of Künssberg's work, which is in most respects identical with the 1925 one, does not, unfortunately, contain these illustrations, but it offers instead a photograph of another defamatory picture.

22. The victim's limbs were broken while he lay on the ground, and he was then attached to the wheel at the top of the post and left to die. The ugly details of this and the other Germanic forms of execution are documented with great thoroughness in Amira 1922.

23. There seems to be some disagreement among the experts as to the exact meaning of the gesture, which is one that occurs again and again in such pictures. Künssberg

The use of pictures to dishonor people was also known in northern
Italy in the later Middle Ages, and some of these representations were
the work of artists of great distinction. In Italy defamatory pictures do
not apparently appear in the context of the pledge of honor but rather
as a method of dishonoring those guilty of very serious offenses.[24]
They seem to have been used above all in cases of treason where the
traitor was out of reach of the authorities. In Central Europe defamatory pictures were instigated by private persons, and imperial legisla-
tion of the sixteenth century and later made a determined attempt to
combat their use; in Italy, in contrast, such pictures were generally produced by order of the public authorities.[25]

Where the loss of honor is marked in a formal way, there is a tendency for the formality, rather than the antecedent misdeed, to be
looked on as what deprives a man of his honor.[26] So in medieval and
early modern Europe the distinction was often made between honorable and dishonorable punishments, the classic instances being respectively beheading and hanging.[27] It is not by chance that the defamatory

---

(1930–31, 602) says that it signifies that excrement is the appropriate wax for a dishonorable signet, whereas Kisch (1931, 518) points out that the creature involved—sow,
cow, mare, female donkey, or bitch—is in all cases female, and writes that the seal is
being pressed against the genitals. It may be, of course, that the artists themselves had
differing views about what they were depicting; Künssberg's theory is perhaps supported
by the fact that the animal is sometimes depicted as excreting. In a picture from the year
1591, a man is represented riding backwards on a naked woman, who is on all fours, and
applying his signet either to her genitals or (as seems more likely) to her anus (Hupp
1930, 83).

24. See Ortalli 1979 and Edgerton 1985, 70–125, both of which give further references.

25. Edgerton 1985, 73 mentions, however, that private defamatory pictures were
often banned by law; so clearly they did exist.

26. Heusler (1885–86, 1:193–94) argues that in German law of the time of the
Rechtsbücher it was not the commission of certain kinds of crime that brought dishonor, but rather conviction for such crimes. Gauvard (1991, 2:887–88) speaks of the
dishonoring effect of punishment inflicted in public in late medieval France.

27. See, for instance, Hirsch 1958, 81; His 1920–35, 1:492–94. German scholars
sometimes distinguish between punishments that humiliate (*Schandstrafen*) and those
that entail the loss of honor (*Ehrenstrafen*). It may be that in the same legal system there
are certain punishments the main point of which is humiliation (e.g., the pillory, dip-
ping, head shaving), but which do not entail loss of honor, and other punishments
which do entail loss of honor; I have not, however, seen a full analysis of such a system,
and the authors of the standard study of the pillory believe that it was a punishment that
always involved loss of honor (Bader-Weiss and Bader 1935, 148–50).

pictures so often represent their targets as being executed: to be executed in a dishonorable fashion—by being hanged by the neck, by being broken on the wheel, by being hanged upside down by one foot[28]—was evidently the ultimate dishonor.[29] The victims in the pictures are mostly noblemen, who as such, if they were to be executed, would almost certainly be beheaded; but representations of beheadings are practically unknown.[30] The notion that certain forms of execution are dishonorable is not confined to medieval Europe: the Romans viewed crucifixion in this way,[31] and it is no doubt as part of the Muslim heritage from the ancient world that the same view appears early on in the history of the caliphate.[32]

At least in some regions of medieval Europe—notably southern Germany and northern Italy—the distinction between honorable and dishonorable punishments corresponded more or less to a distinction between honorable and dishonorable crimes, for example, between killing a man in a fight (honorable) and theft (dishonorable). It was a matter of considerable practical importance what kind of crime one committed; those guilty of honorable crimes had, for instance, much more extensive rights of asylum.[33]

Presumably, the "unhanging" of someone unjustly executed—the ceremony by which the victim's corpse was taken down from the gibbet and transported in procession to where it received a Christian burial[34]—was viewed as the posthumous restoration of honor. In

28. Another punishment especially connected with Jews. Defamatory pictures of this form of execution are first mentioned in Italy in the mid–fourteenth century, and it "was to become the standard form for victims of the art during the next centuries" (Edgerton 1985, 87). Edgerton (1985, 115–18, 120–21) reproduces a series of fine drawings made by Andrea del Sarto in 1530 of a man being hanged upside down.

29. On certain forms of death and of mutilation as sources of dishonor, see also Robreau 1981, 139–40, 143.

30. Hupp 1930, 8.

31. Mommsen 1899, 921.

32. When the sometime governor of Khurasān ʿAbd al-Jabbār b. ʿAbd al-Raḥmān al-Azdī is defeated (probably in A.D. 759) by the caliph, he asks to be killed in an honorable fashion (qitla karīma), but is refused. According to one account, he has a hand and a leg cut off, is killed, and then crucified (al-Balāḏurī 1978, 230); according to another he is first beheaded and then crucified (al-Yaʿqūbī 1883, 2:446). My thanks to Patricia Crone for the references to these passages, and to Michael Lecker for his comments on them.

33. Hirsch 1958, 80–89; His 1920–35, 1:56–60, 2:189; Dahm 1931, 301.

34. Cohen 1993, 196–97 describes a ceremony of this kind that was mounted in Paris in 1304.

Central Europe in the late medieval and early modern period, the executioner—who was normally also responsible for carrying out all bodily punishments—became a figure of the deepest dishonor. Both in the church and in the tavern a special place would often be allotted to him in order to separate him from others.[35] In Basle in about 1546 a drunken artisan proposed to drink with the executioner. The executioner warned him not to, but the artisan insisted. As a result he was expelled from his guild, fell into a deep depression, and ended by committing suicide.[36]

In these circumstances malefactors of sufficient social standing were sometimes able to avoid the dishonor of contact with the executioner by being beheaded (or otherwise punished) by someone else, either as an act of special clemency or by provision of the law.[37] Some inherently dishonoring or humiliating punishments, notably that of being placed in the pillory, were in a number of places divided into a more and a less dishonorable form, according to whether they were inflicted by the executioner or by someone else.[38]

The same tendency to move the stress from the dishonoring deed to the dishonoring formality exists also among the Bedouin. In principle a man loses his honor by (say) failing to fulfill his obligations as a guarantor; but if the obligee fails to blacken him it would, I think, probably be impossible subsequently to convince a court that the man should not be allowed to act as a paid witness.

According to our model personal honor is a matter of all or none; either one has it or one does not, and there are no intermediate points. This is the view of a number of other theorists who have analyzed European honor,[39] and it is true also of Bedouin honor; one does

35. Gernhuber 1957, 127, who notes also that in localities too small to have their own executioner, the visiting executioner was sometimes prohibited from entering a tavern.

36. Osenbrüggen 1969, 134. Compare the regulations of the Franconian nobles mentioned at the beginning of this chapter, and also the dishonoring effect on the British officer of drinking with the private soldiers (chapter 4 above).

37. Gernhuber 1957, 126, 146–47; cf. Dülmen 1990, 67–68. The examples given range from the sixteenth to the eighteenth century.

38. Gernhuber 1957, 146.

39. Thus, for instance, Weinrich 1971, 342 (*die Ehre kennt kein Mehr oder Weniger; man hat die Ehre entweder ganz, oder man hat sie gar nicht*) and Bollnow 1962, 51 (*die Ehre kann nur als Ganze gewahrt oder als Ganze verloren werden*).

not hear of someone who has lost part of his '*ird* and retained part of it.

I take it that this feature of honor is related to the fact that the standards fixed by the honor code, though in some groups they may be very high, are viewed as *minimum* standards. Since they are also extremely important standards, there is often (at any rate, in theory) no such thing as a *minor* infringement of the code: "Whoever offends against the Laws of Honour in the least Instance, is treated as the highest Delinquent."[40] A man who has shown himself to be a coward or a liar, or a woman who is known to have committed adultery, can no longer insist on being treated as a respectable or honest person.

The real world is, of course, much too complicated for any code, and whatever the theory, in practice there are likely to be people who exist in a gray region: ones who are formally dishonorable, but actually widely treated as honorable; ones who are formally honorable, but widely treated as dishonorable; and ones about whose status there is no consensus. 'Aṭiyyih, the Bedouin who tried to prostitute his wife, is a good example: in accepting him as a guarantor, people treat him as if his honor were intact. It is perhaps because of the contrast between theory and practice that the analysts are not always as clear as they might be when they come to this aspect of honor. For example, in his seminal article on the concept of honor in Spain in the sixteenth and seventeenth century, Américo Castro writes at one point that honor "can be acquired or increased in the same way that it can be lost (but not diminished)"; but a few pages later says that to judge by the different modes of revenge that are attested in the drama, "it seems that there is a gradation in the loss of honor, and that the loss is only considered absolute in the case of adultery—whether actual or presumed—by a man's wife."[41]

When the notion of honor falls into the hands of the law, it may undergo a sea change. I have suggested that something of the sort oc-

40. Fielding 1983, 94 (*Amelia,* book 2, chapter 8).
41. Castro 1956, 335, 340. Melveena McKendrick, in commenting on this (in a letter to the author, January 1993), writes, "As to adultery being the only thing that involves absolute loss of honour, I am not so sure; the theatre would certainly suggest that the *mentís* (being called a liar) was taken as seriously. The historical evidence would even suggest that a public *mentís* was actually more harmful than a discreetly wayward wife, for there were many of these and few came to any harm, whereas a non-response to the *mentís* was unthinkable."

curred among the Romans: the simple distinction between the reputable and the disreputable was refined by the jurists, so that in law different types of disreputability brought with them the loss of different civic rights. The same process can be observed in Switzerland in the early modern period; there are instances where individuals are excluded from public office (but not it seems deprived of other civic rights) and where this is explicitly described as a diminution of honor.[42] In Osenbrüggen's view this, and the related phenomenon of temporary dishonor, "shows a misapprehension of the nature of civic honor [*bürgerliche Ehre*], which is no longer viewed as a whole whose offshoots are particular rights, but only as a composite of rights, the loss of which is an impoverishment, like the payment of a fine."[43] Osenbrüggen's view is also my own, and though the Swiss laws in question use the word 'honor', it is not personal honor as the term is understood in this book.

Closely connected with the idea that honor is a matter of all or none is the idea that "honour is like glass—once broken it cannot be mended."[44] I presume that in most systems one who is *wrongly* dishonored may recover his or her honor. The question then is whether one who is *rightly* dishonored may do so. Once more, if one loses one's honor only for heinous offenses, then it makes sense that the loss should be irrecoverable. But each system must be examined in detail to see how far this ruthless logic is followed through. It is said that even the Spanish theater of the Golden Age views honor as something that can be restituted.[45] Certainly in Calderón's *El médico de su honra* it seems to be understood that if Doña Leonor marries Gutierre, with whom she is known to have been associated in compromising circumstances, she

42. Osenbrüggen 1969, 129.
43. Osenbrüggen 1969, 130.
44. Pitt-Rivers 1977, 83. He writes that the Spanish literary tradition repeats this ad nauseam. Unfortunately he gives no references. The comparison is indeed common, but the point being made in the instances that I have come across is not that honor is irreparable, but rather that it is exceedingly fragile. Cf. Castro 1956, 338. Valbuena Briones in a note to Calderón 1956, 11, cites some proverbs to the same effect.
45. Thus Pitt-Rivers 1977, 5, again without references. How this is to be reconciled with the vitreous irreparability of honor is not made clear. Zuckermann-Ingber (1984, 3), in contrast, writes that "once lost, honor could not be regained, and a man's status among his peers was permanently destroyed." This may be true of the material that she is dealing with, but the evidence she cites is not convincing.

will restore her lost honor.[46] Similarly, in the documents relating to certain legal proceedings before an ecclesiastical court in Turin in 1616, a woman is recorded as "insisting, therefore, that the said Francesco be sentenced to marry me in conformity with the promise made, to restore to me the honor taken from me."[47]

The old Swiss laws offer instances of honor that is not merely recoverable, but that is automatically restored after a fairly short time. Osenbrüggen mentions examples of honor being withdrawn for a limited period, anything from six months to three years. He goes on to say that once people began to look on the deprivation of honor, and especially the temporary deprivation of honor, as a punishment, then the proceeding became open to abuse; for instance, a law from Zug recorded in the year 1566 threatens six months' deprivation of honor for those who game by night in a barn with a light.[48] Osenbrüggen says that this shows that honor "had entirely lost its real significance," for in his view someone guilty of a minor misdemeanor of this kind would not have been thought any the worse of by his fellow citizens.[49]

There is nothing in our model of personal honor that excludes the possibility of lost honor being restored. We have, however, stipulated that the rules of the code must be important ones. The lightness of the punishment, if nothing else, shows that the rule about gaming in barns at night was not an important one; and so what the transgressor lost is not personal honor as defined by our model.[50]

There may be a period of time during which a man's honor is moot. Among the Bedouin, for example, when a guest formally draws my

46. See especially 1.683–84. Melveena McKendrick, in commenting on this (in a letter to the author, January 1993), writes that "all the evidence of seventeenth-century Spanish literature shows that the seduced woman *always* regained her reputation and her social identity if she married her seducer—not least because a promise of marriage, even without witnesses, was still regarded as binding in spite of the efforts of the Council of Trent. But of course women, not being full members of society, had no honour that was distinguishable from chastity, and this situation cannot therefore serve as a model for male honour."

47. Cavallo and Cerutti 1990, 76; see also Ferrante 1970.

48. Why precisely this was prohibited is not explained; perhaps because of the risk of setting a fire.

49. Osenbrüggen 1969, 130–31.

50. The tendency to use dishonor as a punishment and to extend it to more and more offenses was a quite general one in the towns of the German-speaking world in the late Middle Ages (Hirsch 1958, 87–88).

Dishonor

attention to the fact that he has been insulted in my home,[51] I am allowed a reasonable amount of time to obtain for him the amends that are his due. My honor is now being put to the test; and after a certain point, the more time goes by without my having done my duty, the more likely it will seem that my honor is failing the test. A day will come when I can be rightfully blackened. The same can happen in other contexts; thus Farrāj, in the protection case mentioned above, found himself in this position, and it could equally happen to a guarantor who does not act promptly after his principal has defaulted.

Such a period of mootness is characteristic of reflexive honor. The Bedouin tend to be quite patient about these things, and the ancient Icelanders were even more so.[52] A Swiss law of the fifteenth century gave a man whose honor was aspersed a year and a day in which to deal with the accusation; after that time he lost his honor.[53] Others are in more of a hurry. In 1900 two German naval officers quarreled while at sea, and one of them slapped the other. The victim waited until the end of the voyage before issuing a challenge and fighting a duel. For this delay he (and his superior officers!) were severely reproved by no less than the Kaiser Wilhelm II himself.[54] The Spaniards of the Golden Age would have met with the imperial approval:

Nunca un español dilata,
la muerte a quien le maltrata,
ni da a su venganza espara.[55]

51. Cf. Stewart 1988–90, 1:1–10.
52. Gehl 1937, 43, 51, 139 n. The cases are, however, not entirely parallel, since among the Bedouin the action by which A redeems his honor is often also one which he has a duty to B to perform, whereas in the typical Icelandic case the action by which A redeems his honor is not one which it is also his duty to another party to perform. Under these circumstances it is not surprising that there should be more pressure on a Bedouin to perform than there was on an Icelander.
53. Osenbrüggen 1969, 125–26.
54. It appears indeed that the victim was forced to resign his commission (Frevert 1989, 568; Frevert 1991, 116).
55. "A Spaniard never delays death to whoever maltreats him, nor does he postpone his revenge." Tirso de Molina, *El celoso prudente*, act 3, scene 6, quoted by Menéndez Pidal 1964, 147 (I have corrected the reference). Similarly, Castro 1956, 334 (*Cuando se llega a perder el honor, la venganza es empleada inmediatamente*). Melveena McKendrick points out (in a letter to the author, January 1993) that "this does not square with the delayed revenges in Calderón's plays, which goes to show how tricky literary evidence is to deal with."

127

One of the most stimulating articles on Arab honor to have appeared in recent years is Wikan 1984.[56] Using data from Cairo and from Oman, the author suggests, among other things, "First that, at least for some people of the Mediterranean and the Middle East, it is *shame* rather than honour which is the predominant concern. Secondly, it is not self-evident that honour is the binary opposite of shame. For some societies, there is evidence that shame contrasts more significantly with other concepts."[57]

The first claim is rather difficult to test as it stands, but we can easily rephrase it as a lexical hypothesis (and indeed Wikan's own treatment of the subject is largely lexical): such and such a people more often uses certain words (which we specify) that mean 'shame' or something similar than they do certain other words (which we also specify) that mean 'honor' or something similar.

What we know of our own society makes this claim decidedly attractive. I think it very likely (for instance) that on any given day the number of times that the English word 'ashamed' is spoken is much greater than the number of times that the word 'honor' is spoken.[58] But the difficulties of rigorously testing such a claim are obvious, and I will not here try to do something of the sort for the Bedouin.[59] I will merely say that I have no intuitive sense of whether the Bedouin concern with honor is more than, or less than, or equal to, their concern with shame; nor have I any intuitive sense of whether they are more or less concerned with shame than we are (if I understand correctly the implication of Wikan's argument, she believes that the societies to which her proposal relates are more concerned with shame than we are). The one thing that I am fairly sure of is that the Bedouin are more concerned with honor than we are.

56. See also Kressel 1988, which is a response to Wikan's article.
57. Wikan 1984, 635–36.
58. Similarly, Brandes 1987, 125.
59. Of course one can quite easily test a claim of this kind not on a whole community, but on a body of recorded material, for example, the Icelandic sagas (cf. Gehl 1937, which offers some interesting statistics about the frequency of occurrence in the various sagas of the various honor words). Indeed, one can instantly test various claims of this type on the texts in Stewart 1988–90, since the glossary of this work lists all occurrences in the texts of a number of words relating to honor and shame; but the relative frequency of such words in the texts is almost certainly quite different from their relative frequency in (let us say) a sample consisting of all that was said by members of the tribe in the year 1980.

Wikan's second thesis—which I take to be that shame is not exactly the opposite of honor—appears to me indisputably correct. Shame is generally looked on as an emotion, whereas honor is not usually regarded as an emotion, and an emotion can scarcely be the exact opposite of something that is not an emotion. The obvious choice for an opposite of shame is pride.[60]

The Bedouin have no exact equivalent of 'dishonor', that is, the opposite of '*ird*. This may be connected with a feature of '*ird* discussed in last part of chapter 12: that it is looked on as a particular thing, like a man's nose; and the opposite of possessing a nose is not possessing an anti-nose, but merely *not* possessing a nose. If a man has lost his '*ird*, then the Bedouin can simply say of him "he has no '*ird*" (*ma lah 'arḍ*).

Arabic in general, and the Bedouin dialect in particular, has a rich vocabulary of words relating to shame, embarrassment, disgrace, and humiliation.[61] In discussing the Cairenes, the shame word to which Wikan pays almost exclusive attention is '*ayb*, which means 'shameful behavior'.[62] This word is also commonly used by the Bedouin,[63] and is probably the closest thing there is to the antithesis of '*ird*: the judges whose task it is to deal with cases involving '*ird*, the Manshads, are also known as the *ahl al-'ayb* 'the people of shameful behavior'.[64] Nevertheless, '*ayb* differs from an antithesis of '*ird* in at least two major respects. First, '*ayb* covers a wider range: it no doubt includes every kind of behavior that would destroy a man's '*ird*, but it also includes much other improper behavior. Second, '*ayb* means 'something shameful, disgraceful': one says of something a person has said or done that it is '*ayb*. But '*ird* never means 'something honorable', and one cannot say of something that a person has said or done that it is '*ird*.

60. See the useful analysis in Taylor 1985.
61. A number of such words are noted in Kressel 1992b (= Kressel 1992a, 195–216).
62. Hinds and Badawi 1986, 611, who also give the sense "defect, fault, flaw." The word exists in much the same sense both in literary Arabic and in many dialects. The reader may gain from Wikan's article the impression that '*ayb* can also mean 'shame', that is, the emotion of shame. This is not so; Arabic has other words for this emotion.
63. Stewart 1988–90, 2:202.
64. Stewart 1988–90, 2:202.

12

BEDOUIN-EUROPEAN CONTRASTS

HONOR AND STRATIFICATION

In the West, honor has usually been closely linked to the class system. This link has manifested itself in many ways. One is in the right enjoyed by the superior classes to the respect of their inferiors. Another is that honor—at least under that name—has often been confined largely or entirely to the higher classes: "Anybody could possess reputation, but only men of some rank could possess honour."[1] Here what is meant is not just vertical honor—for then the statement would practically be true by definition—but also personal honor. It is partly for this reason, and not only because of the bias of the sources, that so much of the evidence relating to European personal honor concerns the elite. Yet there is no doubt that the great mass of the population, the peasants, also believed that people have a right to respect. In the medieval records of the English manorial courts, cases of slander are common.[2] Furthermore, dishonor or shame[3] often appears in these records in quite other contexts. In 1258, for instance, in the court of the Abbot of Ramsey at Broughton in Huntingdonshire, Roger Eyre sues Elias of Stratford, alleging that he "took and drove off four of his oxen wrongfully and detained them on Wednesday next before Michaelmas."[4] Roger demands amends "for damage and shame," a standard formula that appears again and again in all kinds of disputes.[5] Sometimes separate sums are assessed for damage and for shame.[6] In Germany, the peasant law codes (*Weistümer*) leave little doubt that in

1. Barber 1985, 18.
2. Maitland 1974; Maitland and Baildon 1891 (in both works the references are given in the Index of Matters, s.v. "slander"); Sharpe n.d., 32 n. 28; and above all Helmholz 1985, xlviii–lxv, 28–39.
3. In Latin *pudor, dedecus, vituperium;* in French *huntage.*
4. Maitland 1974, 56.
5. Maitland 1974, Index of Matters, s.v. "dishonour and damage" (add to the references given there p. 151); Maitland and Baildon 1891, Index of Matters, s.v. "shame and damage" (there are also many occurrences that are not indexed).
6. This is generally the case in the material in Maitland and Baildon 1891.

the late Middle Ages and in early modern times peasants frequently fought duels about matters of honor.[7] I do not know, however, whether the people in the examples just given used in reference to these disputes a word or phrase meaning honor. Elsewhere, in contrast, the evidence is unequivocal: both in France and in the Low Countries, in the fifteenth century, quite humble people are mentioned as having honor.[8] The independent villagers of the German-speaking parts of Switzerland also saw each other as having honor, and indeed the whole notion was highly developed among them.[9] It has recently been said of early modern Dijon that its "artisans and vignerons knew they possessed honor, even if the upper classes failed to acknowledge it,"[10] and much the same seems to have been true not only of the craftsmen and shopkeepers of Rome of the same period,[11] but even of those lower on the social scale.[12] English people of modest social standing were exceedingly concerned about defamation in the late sixteenth and seventeenth century,[13] though here, as in the instances mentioned in the preceding sentence, it is again not clear to me whether the people in question saw themselves as having honor under that name (or under any other).

A distinguished historian of the old South has gone so far as to write that "when society has pretensions that there are no ranks, honor must necessarily be set aside or drastically redefined to mean something else."[14] Wyatt-Brown seems to be suggesting that honor exists only in societies with well-marked distinctions between social classes. A similar theory has been advanced by one of the best-known anthropologists to have written about Mediterranean honor: "honour is chiefly related to wealth—is an idiom in which differences in wealth are expressed. From these differences are derived differences in honour:

7. Fehr 1908, 25–26.
8. Gauvard 1991, 2:705; Muchembled 1991, 66–68.
9. Osenbrüggen 1969, 111–38 offers an excellent account that is based on the legal sources.
10. Farr 1988, 179.
11. Burke 1987, 106.
12. Cohen 1992, which also gives reference to other works on nonaristocratic honor in early modern Europe.
13. Sharpe n.d. (a very suggestive study, published about 1980).
14. Wyatt-Brown 1982, 14. Unfortunately, the author does not offer his own definition of honor.

poor people have less honour than richer ones and may therefore be insulted, treated as dishonourable, without damage to the honour of their superiors [. . .] The essential characteristics of honour are first that it is a system of stratification: it describes the distribution of wealth in a social idiom."[15]

These views are hard to reconcile with the evidence from the Sinai Bedouin whom I studied, among whom social classes can scarcely be said to have existed. There were, to be sure, differences in wealth, and at the extremes they were considerable: the poorest families each had property worth only a few hundred dollars, while the land and stock of the richest were worth several tens of thousands. But honor, as we have indicated, was in essence equally distributed among all adult men,[16] and to the extent that one can talk about differences in honor, they were not based on wealth. Certain men were known to be more punctilious about their obligations than others, but these were not necessarily rich men. I have mentioned that the men who most frequently put their honor at stake by acting as guarantors or protectors were the leading men; and the leading men tended to be (by Bedouin standards) reasonably well-off. But it was not this that made them leaders, and one of them was in fact thought to be rather poor. Furthermore, the two richest tribesmen whom I knew were not leading men, probably partly because their talents did not lie in that direction, and partly because the agnatic groups to which they belonged were not strong.

The fact that honor among the Bedouin is not connected with class differences is perhaps reflected in their vocabulary. In literary Arabic there are two words that are commonly translated 'honor', *'ird* and *sharaf*. The word *sharaf*, both in the classical and the modern literary language, has not only the sense of 'honor' but also the sense of 'elevation, eminence, high rank'; it resembles the words for honor in the major modern European languages in that it often relates to both vertical and horizontal honor. *'Ird*, in contrast, carries no suggestion of vertical honor. In many dialects both words are used, often in somewhat different ways. It is noteworthy that *sharaf* and related words from the same root are rarely used by the Aḥaywāt in any sense to do with honor

15. Davis 1977, 91, 98. Cf. Pitt-Rivers 1968, 507: "Honor is always bound to wealth and possessions."
16. Contrast Davis 1977, 110: "Systems of honour are wrongly called egalitarian by their ethnographers."

or rank; and when they are so used, it is, I suspect, the result of outside influence.[17] The absence of the word *sharaf* may reflect the fact that the Bedouin are in many ways markedly egalitarian,[18] and that the most prominent kind of honor among the Bedouin is horizontal rather than vertical.

HONOR AND OBLIGATIONS

It is not merely verbal insults and blows that Europeans connect with honor. In mid–twentieth century Sicily, "honour is at stake whenever property rights are wilfully infringed [. . .] when livestock or crops have been stolen, when part of the harvest is damaged, when cattle, sheep or goats are driven through another man's pastures or fields (*pascolo abusivo*) or when fruit-trees or vines have been cut down. In all these cases the honour of the owner, proprietor or guard is impugned."[19] We can go back in time to the very beginning of the Middle Ages, to the far western edge of Europe, and discover ideas that are not strikingly different. In early Irish law "the measure of a person's status is his honour-price or *lóg n-enech* (lit. 'the price of his face'). This had to be paid for any major offence committed against him, e.g. murder, satire, serious injury, refusal of hospitality, theft, violation of his protection, etc."[20] (The honor price was in addition to the amends that were due for the offense itself.)

Almost all this is alien to the Bedouin. If you hit him, he can in law either hit you back or get blood money; either way, '*ird* has nothing to do with it. If you make off with his camel without his permission, a court will order you to return him his camel and to give him four

17. *Sharaf* does not occur in the texts in Stewart 1988–90; see Stewart 1988–90, 2:269. The fact that it is probably not part of the dialect—though it is occasionally used—should have been noted in Stewart 1988–90, 2:20 n, where the term *kalām sharaf* 'word of honor' is mentioned. The word *sharīf* 'honorable', though it occurs once in the texts, is also probably not a local word (and again, this should have been indicated).

18. See, for instance, Stewart 1988–90, 1:3 (Text 2), where a man expresses forcefully the principle that the sheikh and the ordinary tribesman are equal before the law.

19. Blok 1981, 433. In this passage Blok writes also of property rights being willfully infringed "when the chastity of a woman is violated." Perhaps at some very general and abstract level the rights that Sicilian men have in their womenfolk resemble those that they have in their goats; but at the more day-to-day level of buying and selling goats, stealing goats, tying goats up for the night, shipping goats hither and thither, slaughtering goats, and the like, I assume—and I certainly hope—that there are marked differences.

20. Kelly 1988, 8.

others by way of amends; if you allow your camels to eat his crop, you will have to pay him amends; but it will not cross anyone's mind in either case that the victim's *'ird* has been involved. In fact there is *nothing* you can do directly to a Bedouin that will constitute a primary impugnment of his *'ird*. This is because his *'ird* is never at stake when he is merely defending himself or his property, but only when he acts[21] (*a*) in the context of a sexual offense against his ward, or (*b*) in the context of a duty that he owes to another person.

a) It is only *sexual* offenses against a man's ward that involve his *'ird*. If someone hits or insults a man's sister or daughter it is, of course, an offense against him, but it is not an offense against his *'ird*. On the other hand, Bedouin ideas of what constitutes a sexual offense are much broader than our own. The Bedouin look on every woman rather in the way that we look on a female below the age of consent; that is to say, the fact that the woman consented to the sexual activity does not make it legitimate (though it may well constitute a mitigating circumstance when it comes to deciding what amends are due).[22] Furthermore, it is not only the grosser forms of sexual activity that entail liability; for instance, it is an offense for a young man to have a flirtatious conversation with a young woman not his wife, and it is an offense for a man wrongly to accuse his wife of infidelity (even if there are no witnesses to the accusation). And finally, it is not even clear that the offender need have sexual intentions; when a man in the course of a scuffle with some other men accidentally caused the veil to fall from the face of his niece, her guardian raised claims to a manshad, though it was never suggested that the uncle's action had been anything but an accident.

When a sexual offense is committed against a woman, a triangular structure is established that is represented in figure 2 (see p. 144 below). This triangle obviously resembles those in figure 1, yet there are two striking differences. First, the disputes represented in figure 1 are trilateral, while the dispute in figure 2 is in legal terms bilateral, between the offender and the guardian. The guardian has no legal duties

21. Or forbears to act. In what follows I shall use the word 'act' and its cognates to include forbearance.

22. Perhaps I should add that my impression is that though what the Bedouin look on as sexual offenses are extremely common among them, only a tiny minority of such offenses are carried out without the woman's consent.

to his ward, and the ward has no right to blacken her guardian.[23]
Second, in the cases represented in figure 1 the man on the bottom
right-hand corner is normally doing something to the man on the bottom
left-hand corner that the latter objects to; whereas the ward usually consents to the action by the offender.

b) All the other cases in which a man's *'ird* is at stake, though very
varied, have the common feature that the man has an obligation (frequently one that he has assumed of his own free will), and that it is a
failure to meet this obligation that will lead to his being dishonored
(and hence open to being blackened). This is true both of the bipartite
cases mentioned in chapter 7 and of the tripartite ones discussed in
chapter 8.

A sexual offense against a man's ward (fig. 2) or the violation of a
man's protection (fig. 1, item 3—see p. 98 above) always constitutes a
primary impugnment of a man's *'ird*. In contrast, an obligor who defaults (fig. 1, item 2) does not thereby impugn the guarantor's *'ird*, and
a man who violates the peace of a home (fig. 1, item 1) does not in
most cases impugn the *'ird* of the master of the home. Some suggestions can be made as to why these different breaches of duty are treated
in different ways, but the subject is complex and a discussion would
take us beyond the bounds of the present work.

The fact that Bedouin *'ird* rests (roughly speaking) on the proper fulfillment of certain duties to another party is closely connected with the
sharp distinction between a primary impugnment and a blackening.
To understand the connection, we can begin by imagining how things
would be if blackening did not exist. Let us assume that I am injured
while a guest in Sālim's home, and that circumstances make it impossible for me, without Sālim's assistance, to get justice from my assailant. Sālim now has a duty to assist me; but let us further assume that
he fails to do so. In order to get my due I am going to have to sue him.
Sālim, however, may not be eager to defend himself in court, and while
Bedouin law provides a procedure for forcing a reluctant defendant to

23. It may well be that if a guardian were to take no action regarding a sexual offense
against his ward, then her other agnates would have a right to blacken him; if this, or
something of the sort, were true, it would make the structure in figure 2 much more
similar to the structures in figure 1. Unfortunately, I have no information that bears
directly on this point; the facts referred to in Stewart 1987a, 46, are, however, suggestive.

appear before a judge, it is a lengthy and difficult one: the plaintiff must summons the defendant in person and in his home on three different occasions, each time bringing with him four witnesses; only if this produces no results may the plaintiff then levy distraint upon the defendant's camels. Given the mobility of the Bedouin, and given the fact that Sālim (and perhaps his kinsmen) will resist the seizure, the chances of my carrying out this procedure are slim. It is open to me, of course, to go around telling people how Sālim let me down, and with luck this will have a bad effect on his reputation. But of course Sālim will have his own version of what happened, which he will also be propagating, and people may be just as likely to believe him as they are to believe me; many will no doubt say that the whole matter is unclear. And even if it should happen that everyone believes me and not Sālim, I will still not have received amends for my injury.

Blackening offers a solution to this unsatisfactory state of affairs. I wrote originally (chapter 7) that it is like an accusation that a man has done something that dishonors him; but it is not *exactly* like an accusation. An accusation is something that may be believed or disbelieved; but one cannot believe or disbelieve a blackening. One might say that when first done it is like an indictment; and that if the man against whom it is directed does not obtain a manshad from his blackener within a reasonable time, then from being an indictment it turns into a verdict. But it is not quite like a verdict either. Public opinion can accept a verdict or reject it, but it cannot accept or reject a blackening: the deed is done, the man is dishonored. There is no analogy here to the contrast between 'he is guilty' and 'he has been found guilty'. A man who has been blackened resembles an officer who is stripped of his commission: provided that the proper procedures have been followed, we have to accept, whether we like it or not, that (say) Captain Dreyfus is now plain M. Dreyfus.

There is something not quite logical about the blackening, and for this reason it is perhaps best characterized in a paradoxical fashion: it is a means by which A may dishonor B; yet A can dishonor B in this way only if B has already dishonored himself by failing to meet an obligation of honor that he has to A. But whatever its logical shortcomings, the practical advantages of the procedure are manifest: it gives A a powerful and easily deployed sanction that he can use to force B either to carry out his obligation or to take the matter to court; and if B refuses to do either, then at least A will have dishonored B.

Let us now compare the operation of honor among the upper classes in Europe. One can, if one wishes, draw a distinction between primary impugnments on the one hand and accusations of dishonorable behavior on the other. One example of a primary impugnment would be an adulterous relationship with a man's wife; another would be an insult that does not imply dishonorable behavior. The remarks directed, for instance, at the unhappy Captain Beilby (chapter 2 above) seem to have arisen from the way that he handled his men—another of them was said to have been "is that the way you make your men slope their arms, you dirty dog?" There is no indication that he was being accused of having done anything dishonorable. An example of an accusation that someone has acted in a way that destroys his honor would be, "You have been cheating at cards." But the distinction between primary impugnments and accusations of dishonorable behavior is of no particular significance. Either, for instance, might give rise to a challenge. There is, moreover, nothing quite like the Bedouin blackening. The reason why can be illustrated from the events surrounding a famous German duel that took place in the year 1887.

Willy von Liebermann, an aristocratic Jew, believed that he had been insulted during his army service by his senior officer, and that the officer had been motivated by anti-Semitism. As long as he was a soldier, Liebermann could do nothing; but the very day be completed his year in the army, Liebermann challenged the officer to a pistol duel under conditions that made it distinctly likely that injury or death would result from the encounter. The officer refused to accept the challenge, and referred the matter to a military tribunal of honor (*Ehrenrat*). The *Ehrenrat* did not want to authorize the duel, and tried to encourage a peaceful settlement. But Liebermann was adamant: he let it be understood that if necessary he would force the officer to accept by assaulting (*tätlich beleidigen*) him on the street when he (the officer) was in uniform. The *Ehrenrat* was left with no choice but to sanction the duel, which then took place.[24]

The kind of assault that Liebermann threatened was evidently a purely symbolic one, a slap in the face or something similar. Functionally, this was like threatening a blackening: either the officer would

24. Liebermann von Wahlendorf 1988, 55–64. Liebermann emerged from the encounter unscathed, but the officer was seriously injured. This was only one of four pistol duels that Liebermann fought, and much is to be learned about contemporary German notions of honor from his autobiography.

be forced to give Liebermann what Liebermann claimed to be his due (an apology), or he would be forced to challenge him to a duel (the European analogue of suing Liebermann before the Manshad), or, if he did neither, the officer would be dishonored.[25] But the slap in the face has none of the logical complexity of the blackening: it is simply a primary impugnment.

If a European can achieve his ends with the mere threat of a primary impugnment, why cannot a Bedouin do the same? The answer is clear: among the Bedouin no action taken directly against a man is a primary impugnment of his honor. A Bedouin Liebermann would have to threaten to commit a sexual offense against the officer's sister or to threaten to harm some interest of a third party that had been placed under the officer's protection. The reasons for not doing this kind of thing are obvious. So instead of using primary impugnments, the Bedouin resort to blackening, an institution whose whole oddity arises from the fact that it is a device whose purpose is to allow one man directly to dishonor another that exists in a system in which one man *cannot* directly dishonor another.

One final observation suggests itself. Let us assume that the *Ehrenrat* had refused to approve the duel, that Liebermann had indeed slapped the officer on the face, and that the officer had then challenged Liebermann to a duel. Liebermann would have achieved some of what he wanted in this way, but not quite all. Formally speaking, the duel would then not have been about the insults that Liebermann suffered, but about the insult that the officer suffered, and the officer would have been the challenger (or insultee) rather than the challenged (or insulter), a fact which under some dueling codes might have important implications.[26] Even in the European system, then, the use of primary impugnments in this way leads to certain logical and practical difficulties.

The Bedouin blackening, in contrast, leads to precisely the relevant issue being tried. If Bedouin B sues Bedouin A for wrongfully blackening him, then the court will decide whether B did in fact act dishonorably; and if B loses his case, he will recover his honor by giving A his due.

25. It is evident that if the officer had apologized to Liebermann he would have been humiliated, but it does not seem that such an apology would have dishonored him.
26. Cf. Mader 1983, 52–53.

Honor and Violence

Under a system of reflexive honor, a man's honor depends, by definition, on his responding properly each and every time that his honor is challenged. In a society where honor may be viewed as more valuable than life itself, it would be intolerable if honor could continually be challenged under trivial pretexts. Both in Europe and among the Bedouin, this danger is obviated by the severity of the counterattack that a man will mount in order to retain his honor. The difference is that in Europe he very often retains his honor by trying to kill the man who impugned it, whereas among the Bedouin he does so by getting from him a massive award at law.

Bedouin law is, as one might expect, fundamentally directed towards the peaceful settlement of disputes, and it uses a variety of devices, some of them exceedingly subtle, to discourage the use of force. Since the notion of 'ird is incorporated into the legal system, any dispute about 'ird that runs its full course will end with a hearing before the Manshad. But there are certain areas in which even the law has to legitimate violent behavior, and one is in connection with sexual offenses. If you have (let us say) seduced my daughter, then you and all the other men in your blood-money group are now lawful targets for me and the men in my group: we may seize whatever we can lay our hands on of your property, and whatever physical harm we inflict on you, short of actual homicide, will not entail any liabilities for us. In practice it may not be easy for us to find you: you and your men, together with all your movable property, will have fled and concealed yourselves. After a certain amount of time you will begin sending us emissaries, asking us to give you a truce; and eventually, upon payment of an appropriate sum of money (the *jīrih*),[27] we will give you such a truce. You can then safely return to your normal existence, and arrangements will be made for the case to be heard by a Manshad. We will be entitled to retain any property we have seized from you, and in addition we will receive a manshad, that is, substantial amends.

There is also another side to violence in the context of sexual offenses. Bedouin law gives the guardian the power of life and death over his ward. He can beat her severely or even kill her, and if she has been

27. Stewart 1988–90, 2:239.

unchaste the idea of punishing her for it is not unknown to the Bedouin. But law and custom also include elements whose effect is to protect the ward. I knew of three unmarried Aḥaywāt women who became pregnant, and none suffered any physical harm from her guardian.[28] The killing of an unchaste woman by her father or brother is, however, to this day practiced in some Arab communities,[29] and it would not surprise me if it happened sometimes among Bedouin who have essentially the same legal system as the Aḥaywāt.

To put the matter in perspective, I should emphasize that only a minority of ʿird disputes among the Bedouin involve sexual offenses, and of that minority a considerable number are settled without resort to violence. The law *permits* the use of violence in certain contexts; it never *demands* it. Violence, whether directed against the man or against the woman, does not cleanse a man's ʿird:[30] the only thing that will do this is a manshad.

In Europe and the New World, violence played a far more prominent role in affairs of honor than it does among the Bedouin. A character in a Spanish drama described honor as "something invisible that feeds on blood."[31] The sword is often the symbol par excellence of honor, and the old Swiss records, for instance, are full of phrases like *Ehr und Gewehr* 'honor and weapon,' *ehrlos und gewehrlos* 'without honor and without weapon,' and its opposite, *ehrhaft und wehrhaft.*[32] Mediation and even litigation might resolve some disputes,[33] but in

28. Bailey (1991, 21) is guilty of a gross exaggeration when he writes of "the mandatory murder of errant girls" among the Sinai Bedouin.

29. See for instance Kressel 1981, reprinted with minor revisions in Kressel 1992a, 160–94.

30. There is a single exception to this: when a husband kills his wife's lover (a relatively common event) he is said to have "whitened himself." This is the one case where notions of honor appear outside the legal system (since in law it is not the husband, but the guardian, who is offended by the lover).

31. *Es una cosa invisible / Que de sangre se sustenta* (Guillén de Castro, *El nacimiento de Montesinos,* quoted in Castro 1956, 338).

32. Osenbrüggen 1969, 111–16; and for further references, see the relevant entries in the *Deutsches Rechtswörterbuch.*

33. Especially, perhaps, among the lower classes. To take a single example, Sharpe concludes (*a*) "that it *was* felt necessary to respond to insults, whether by violence or by waging war" (this suggests a reflexive system), and (*b*) that in dealing with insults, "the Englishman of that period regarded a suit at law as an acceptable alternative to violence" (Sharpe n.d., 23–24). The sources used by Sharpe deal mainly with people below the gentry (Sharpe n.d., 17); the growing popularity during this period of the duel, which

many cases nothing short of a physical attack would do: whether the knight on horseback tilting at his opponent with a lance, the Icelander hacking down his foe with ax or sword, the Spaniard doing away with the wife whom be believes has deceived him, or the duelist confronting his opponent pistol in hand at dawn. There is a certain logic behind much of this, and as regards the errant wife it is a logic that the Bedouin would be quick to recognize: the source of the dishonor is punished and destroyed.[34] The logic for men may be the same, or it may be somewhat different. As we have seen, in much of Europe, during the Middle Ages, quite simply victory brought honor, and defeat dishonor. And one can find other justifications; for instance, by doing away with the man who dishonored me, or (as often in the medieval epics) by reducing him to abjectly begging for his life, I effectively stop him from ever dishonoring me again, I show myself superior to him in at least one important way, and I produce a deterrent effect on others who might be tempted to behave like him. If, on the other hand, my enemy kills me, at least I am no longer going to be worried about my honor; and if he merely humbles me—well, he will have done that already even if I do not fight him.

But this is not all. Rudyard Kipling, in the story mentioned in chapter 11, lets it be known both that the officer could have apologized in private to the soldier, and that such an apology would not have provided a satisfactory resolution. The element of privacy is apparently not significant: the fistfight also took place in private. In a normal European affair of honor, an apology in the proper form will avert a duel, but in this particular case, I would guess, it is excluded because it might have a flavor of *de haut en bas*. Now none of the considerations that are mentioned in the preceding paragraph apply here: the need for violence seems to arise from a sense—not uncommon in Western popular literature—that for one man to engage in a fistfight with another is to give each an opportunity to prove his worth to the other, not by winning, but by showing pluck. The victim of the insult, the soldier, is

---

was confined to the higher ranks of society, suggests that litigation was less acceptable to the elite. Yet even among gentlemen "scandalous words provocative of a duel" might in the early seventeenth century lead to a lawsuit rather than a fight (Squibb 1959, 37–38, 57–61).

34. The Bedouin, of course, would apply this logic to a ward, not to a wife. I knew of four cases where a jealous husband killed a man he believed to be his wife's lover, but I never heard of a wife being killed (and indeed not one of these four wives was even divorced).

saying, as it were, "You treated me like dirt. Very well: now I will see to it that you deal with me as one man deals with another." And perhaps also, "You behaved badly: now regain my respect by behaving well in difficult circumstances." This last thought would be another reason why an apology was not in place here.

The logic of violence, be it what it may, looks rather crude if one compares it to the Bedouin way of doing things, which is to try the dispute before an impartial judge. It has been said that "the concept of Mediterranean honour is still primarily contingent on physical strength and bearing, especially so in small-scale rural communities in peripheral and mountainous areas."[35] The Bedouin, at any rate, know nothing of this. Among them power and respect gravitate to sharp-witted men with self-confident, independent personalities. These are the leaders, the men whose honor is most heavily engaged: they are the ones who are constantly giving guarantees, entertaining large gatherings, offering protection, and the like; and they are mostly middle-aged or elderly. As their mental faculties decline in very old age, their influence will diminish, but people are no more interested in their physical strength and bearing than we are in the physical strength and bearing of a senator, a lawyer, or a federal appeals court judge.

The rationality of the Bedouin procedure becomes even more apparent if it is compared to the European (and New World) duel in its later form. Karl Binding, a leading criminalist of Wilhelmine Germany, postulated the following case: a scoundrel (of good family) cold-bloodedly seduces and abandons a young girl (also of good family). She and her family have suffered terrible harm, but the law offers no redress: she has passed her sixteenth birthday, and thus reached the age of consent. Her father challenges the seducer to a duel. He may kill the scoundrel—if not a wholly desirable, yet at any rate a reasonable, outcome. But what if the seducer survives the duel? Even if he is defeated he is recognized as having retained his honor; and if he wins, not only will he retain his honor, he will also have added to the family's misery by killing or wounding the father.[36] Binding, who proposed the re-

<hr>

35. Blok 1981, 432. Cf. Pitt-Rivers (1968, 505): "The body as a whole is especially associated with honor [. . .] honor centers in the physical being."

36. Binding 1909, 55–62. (This volume consists of the texts of two lectures, *Die Ehre und ihre Verletzbarkeit*, given in 1890, and *Der Zweikampf und das Gesetz*, given in 1905). The arguments that can be mustered in favor of the duel may be found, for instance, in Reiner 1956, 62–68. He discusses the case of the seduced girl on pp. 75–77.

placement of the duel by special courts of honor (*Ehrengerichte*),[37] would no doubt have been favorably impressed by the Manshad.

It was not very long after Binding's time that the duel became extinct, even in Germany. Whether his lectures had much to do with this is another matter. Binding was no more than a late representative of a line stretching back centuries: the arguments against the use of violence to settle disputes of honor had always been most convincing—and yet the world went its way.

'Honor' and '*Ird*

So far I have considered substantive differences between Bedouin ideas about honor and European ones. I want to end with some brief remarks about what might be called lexical differences between the way the word 'honor' is used and the way the word '*ird* is used.

The word '*ird* has a far narrower range of meanings than the English noun 'honor' or its equivalents in other major modern European languages. Apart from its use in a few special expressions,[38] it clearly means one thing and one thing only; a lexicographer is faced with no problems of classification, for there is nothing like the immense number of shades of meaning that the word 'honor' has in English. Moreover, there is only one kind of Bedouin '*ird*. 'Honor', even when it is used in a narrow sense that parallels '*ird*, can be applied to things that are clearly different from each other: the honor of a man, of a woman, of a peer, and so on. These kinds of honor have different bases and express themselves in different ways. In contrast, '*ird* refers exclusively to a single kind of honor, the one that is allotted to all and only the men in the community.

In English (as in other major modern European languages) honor is frequently spoken of separately from its particular bearer, as when we say that something is a matter of honor, that honor is sometimes found among thieves, that the agreement with the Ruritanians has brought peace with honor, or that honor is worth more than life itself.[39] The Bedouin of central Sinai rarely use the word '*ird* in this kind of general sense.[40] They look on a man's '*ird* as a thing that he pos-

37. Binding 1909, 66–67.

38. Stewart 1988–90, 2:199.

39. The common phrase 'man of honor' (and the like) also falls under this heading: cf. 'man of wealth', 'man of strength', 'man of importance', etc.

40. I have in fact not yet noted any unambiguous examples of such usage (in partic-

sesses. The word occurs twenty-three times in Stewart 1988–90, and every single instance is in the context 'N's honor', where N is a proper name or a pronoun.[41] That a man's honor is looked on as a particular thing (like his mouth or his nose) may also be seen from another contrast: in modern English (as in other major modern European languages), speaking of two men, we say "their honor," just as we say "their strength," even if the honor of each one is wholly independent of that of the other; but the Bedouin, though they say "their strength" (*guwwithum*), say "their honors" (*'rūdhum*). In this the Bedouin resemble not only their own ancestors,[42] but also the English of the seventeenth century. At that time 'honor', in the sense that concerns us here, was like *'ird* a count noun;[43] and this fits well with the fact that in the drama of the period honor "is often spoken of as if it were a kind of chattel, like the owner's other wordly goods."[44]

Finally, it is noteworthy that the Bedouin do not use *'ird* in a way that might lead one to think that *'ird* is a virtue. To be sure, a sentence like 'he has no *'ird*' (*ma lah 'ard*) offers a setting in which *'ird* could usually, without inconsistency with the context, be interpreted as referring to a virtue, but there is nothing in most uses of *'ird* to lead one to believe that this is in fact what *'ird* is. In other words, the possibility of stressing the internal aspect of the claim-right is not exploited. The same thing was also true at one time in Europe, where 'honor' was frequently used to refer to a right long before it was frequently used with an internal sense.

---

ular, no instances in which *'ird* is preceded by the definite article). Jaussen 1948, 204 n gives an example of such a usage in a proverb from the Bedouin of Transjordania.

41. The same is true of the examples of the use of *'ird* given in Kressel 1992b (= 1992a, 195–216); he includes a number of interesting expressions that I did not encounter in central Sinai.

42. Various examples of the use of *a'rāḍ*, the classical Arabic plural of *'ird*, are given in Farès 1932, 37.

43. For instance, in Shakespeare's *Troilus and Cressida*, II.2.123–24: "a quarrel / which hath our several honours all engag'd." Cf. Barber 1957, 48.

44. Barber 1957, 101.

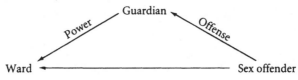

Figure 2

13

CONCLUSION

The more closely one looks at honor, the odder it seems. Honor is very important—more important than life itself, it is often said[1]—yet a man can be in a state of dishonor without realizing it. Honor is the reward of virtue, so the old books tell us again and again; yet a virtuous man can be dishonored through no fault of his own. Someone who wrongfully impugns my honor (by insulting me, by seducing my daughter, or whatever) may have to pay a price for it—but he has not thereby acted dishonorably. The duel, a practice that in the face of every effort to stamp it out flourished and spread for a period of centuries, is a patently irrational way of settling disputes. Even blackening someone's face, an admirable institution in its context, turns out to have logical peculiarities.

In these circumstances it is perhaps not surprising that the analyses of honor that have been proposed are sometimes so different from each other that one would not suspect, if one did not already know, that they relate to the same concept (or, at any rate, the same word).[2]

I have mainly been concerned with *personal honor*, that is, the kind of honor that we would usually have in mind if we were to say, for instance, 'my honor' or 'a matter of honor.' The central argument has been that this kind of honor is a right. I have characterized it roughly as a right to respect as an equal; but the question of what honor is a right *to* has been touched on only very lightly. The answer varies from one instance to another, and to generalize is not easy.

I have stipulated that in order to constitute personal honor the right in question must have the following features:
1. It can be lost.
2. In order to retain it one must follow certain rules. These rules are

---

1. This view is expressed again and again in the European sources, and it is also known in the Arab world. Thus Feghali 1938, 77 quotes the proverb "It is better to die with honor [*sharaf*] than to live in humiliation."

2. Even analyses given by the same author are not always easy to reconcile with each other. See, for instance, the quotations from Pitt-Rivers in chapter 2 above.

the *code of honor.* The people who follow the same code of honor and recognize each other as doing so constitute an *honor group.*

3. The honor group has in its language at least one word or phrase that is frequently used to refer to the right in question.

The model should also somehow incorporate the notion that the rules that constitute the code of honor set up standards that are viewed as being of cardinal importance in judging a person's worth. The existence of such standards provides in fact a natural starting point for an analysis of the notion of personal honor. Many societies have such standards, and in many societies people accordingly draw some kind of division between those who are respectable and those who are not respectable (or who are disgraced or despicable). Where this happens those who are respectable have by virtue of this fact rights which those in the other category lack. In certain of the societies that make such a division further developments have taken place: these rights—or at least some of them—have come to be looked on as a single right; that right has been given a name (in English 'honor'); and it has become possible to describe the division as being between those who have this right and those who do not (either because they never had it, or because they once had it but have now lost it).

A man of honor must appear both to understand the code of honor and to be attached to its precepts; such understanding and attachment constitute his *sense of honor.* I have suggested that in the last phase of European honor more and more stress was laid on the individual's sense of honor, and less and less on the particular code that he or she followed; and that there is some connection between this and the decline in the importance of honor.

The idea that honor is a right has been suggested before (in the German juridical literature); but it has not hitherto been appreciated how powerful an idea it is. I have tried to show that it can help resolve what came to be the central paradox in European honor, the contrast between inner and outer honor.[3] The details demand further investiga-

3. The notion that honor is a right originally came to me when I was looking for a solution to this paradox, and it was only subsequently that I discovered that others before me had had the same idea. The German jurists, however, came up with the idea in a quite different context; and though they were (and are) well aware of the inner-outer contrast, it does not seem to have occurred to them that the notion of honor as a right might offer a solution to the difficulties that it presents. It is noteworthy that the word

tion, but it would seem that *inner honor* is honor viewed from the point of view of the bearer of the right, or with that in mind which entitles the bearer to the right, and *outer honor* is honor viewed from the point of view of the attitudes and beliefs of those who have the corresponding duty.

The same theory of honor that is so useful in understanding late European honor shows itself to be no less helpful when applied to certain non-European concepts, the Bedouin notions of *'ird* and *wajh* ('face'). In fact the theory fits *'ird* and *wajh* even better than it does 'honor'. The various words that mean 'honor' in the major modern European languages are all used in a wide variety of senses, and the instances in which the special right which I call personal honor is being referred to are not always easy to isolate. The Arabic word *'ird*, in contrast, as it is used by the Bedouin, usually refers to just such a right to respect; and when it is being used in some other way, the difference is perfectly clear. *Wajh* has a much wider range of uses, but here too the occurrences in which it is used with reference to a right to respect are entirely distinct from the others.

The theory presented here is also strongly supported by an analysis of the pledge of honor, an institution found both in Europe and among the Bedouin. It is difficult to imagine how honor, in this institution, can be looked on as anything other than a right.

Two important distinctions have been briefly discussed. One has not hitherto been made in any very explicit fashion, though its existence has clearly been perceived. In every system of honor it is possible to behave towards a man in a way that is inconsistent with his honor. In some systems no particular response is prescribed; but in others, those characterized by what I have called *reflexive honor*, there is an honor code that demands that the man whose honor is impugned mount a counterattack. If he fails to do so, he loses his honor. Reflexive systems tend to look very different from nonreflexive ones, but the exact significance of the distinction remains to be investigated.

The other distinction is in essence a familiar one, though authorities differ both in exactly how they make it and in the terminology they

---

they use to refer to the right in question is *Anspruch*, the central meaning of which is 'claim' rather than 'right'; that is to say, it tends to evoke a one-sided rather than a two-sided notion.

use. I have used the terms 'horizontal honor' and 'vertical honor'. Any right to respect as an equal is an instance of *horizontal honor;* personal honor is therefore a particular type of horizontal honor. An individual who has personal honor may also have additional rights to respect that would be classified as horizontal honor; for instance, if A fails to greet B, where A and B are equals, this may not be looked on as an offense against B's personal honor and yet still be viewed as a failure by A to show B the respect that is his due. *Vertical honor* is the right to special respect enjoyed by those who are superior. The respect due by virtue of the possession of horizontal honor cannot be increased (this is so by definition). In contrast, the respect due by virtue of the possession of vertical honor can sometimes be increased. The words for honor in the major modern European languages refer to both types; in Arabic, however, both in the literary language and in many dialects, one word for honor ('*ird*) refers only to certain kinds of horizontal honor, while another (*sharaf*) may refer either to certain kinds of vertical honor or to certain kinds of horizontal honor or to both.

The notion of horizontal honor can be applied to a society irrespective of the degree to which members of the society are themselves aware of the existence of the rights in question. In this it stands in sharp contrast to the notion of personal honor which (as defined here) refers to a concept that is possessed by the members of the society and for which they have a particular term. Assume that society X has a notion of personal honor, which the people call *dovak*. Part of the notion of *dovak* will be the particular bundle of rights that constitutes its core. Now in another society, call it Y, people have rights similar—let's even say identical—to those in the *dovak* bundle; but society Y does not group these rights together and view them as a whole. Under these circumstances it would not be correct to say that in society Y, even though people do not have a name for *dovak,* they do have the concept itself; and a fortiori it would not be correct to say on the basis of their alleged possession of the notion of *dovak* that they have a concept of personal honor.

Initially (let us say) society X differed from society Y only in that it grouped certain rights together as *dovak;* but once society X has done this, it can go on to use the notion of *dovak* to build a variety of institutions (e.g., the pledge of honor) that will make society X increasingly different from society Y.

The implication of the definitions given of horizontal and vertical honor is that almost all rights to respect are types of honor. It may well turn out, however, that it is a mistake to group these very diverse rights under a single heading.

This essay has also considered the theory that there is a notion of honor shared by the peoples whose territories border the Mediterranean, and distinct from the notions of honor of their inland neighbors. I have advanced two main claims against this idea. One is that northern European honor is not very different from southern European honor: I have suggested that European ideas about honor have changed greatly through time, but that they have not been radically different from one country to another (excepting at certain times marginal regions such as Iceland or Montenegro). The other is that honor among many Bedouin groups *is* very different from European honor, whether northern or southern. The code that a Bedouin must obey in order to retain his honor is different from the one that a European must obey, and the range of actions that constitute an infringement of a Bedouin's honor is different from the range of actions that constitute an infringement of a European's honor; and in both cases the differences are not in matters of detail, but in matters of principle.

I have also suggested that even though many Bedouin live on the borders of the Mediterranean, the Bedouin are not a Mediterranean people in the sense that, say, the Greeks are a Mediterranean people, that is, a people whose life is deeply influenced by their proximity to the inland sea; but I do not believe that a slightly modified theory of Mediterranean honor—that is, one that excluded from its scope the Bedouin and perhaps some other littoral peoples—would stand up any better than the version given above. This is because I am fairly confident (though I have not attempted to prove it here) that ideas about honor among the Arabic-speaking population of the eastern Mediterranean are in general substantially different from European ones and have much in common with the ideas about honor of Arabic-speaking populations to the east and south.

APPENDIX ONE

The History of the Idea of Honor as a Right

The idea that honor is a right enjoyed considerable popularity in German legal circles in the 1950s and 1960s, but then went out of fashion; and it does not seem to have had any influence outside legal circles.[1] The details are as follows. In 1951 a German federal court, dealing with a case of insult, defined honor as "the right of a human being that their personality be respected" (*der Anspruch eines Menschen auf Achtung seiner Persönlichkeit*).[2] This definition was taken word for word (though without acknowledgment) from an article by a distinguished jurist of the Weimar Republic, Eduard Kern.[3] The court (like Kern) offered no arguments or authorities in favor of the definition, but it was nevertheless adopted, with minor variations, by a number of jurists.[4] The *Achtungsanspruch* theory, as it is sometimes called, was attacked by Hans Joachim Hirsch in the first major juristic analysis of honor to be written in the Federal Republic,[5] and then went into decline. Hans Welzel, the author of a popular textbook of German criminal law, who had in some earlier editions embraced the theory, turned his back on the *Achtungsanspruch* theory under Hirsch's influence;[6] the author of the next book-length study of honor in German law dismissed the theory with a few words;[7] Schönke-Schröder, a standard commentary on the German penal code, which in a number of editions had adopted the *Achtungsanspruch* theory, came to take a different view;[8] and in a decision handed down in 1989 the federal court itself no longer speaks of honor as a right to respect, but rather as something in virtue of which one has a right to respect (*der aus Ehre fliessende verdiente Achtungsanspruch*).[9]

The arguments that have been brought against the *Achtungsanspruch* theory by German jurists[10] are in part shaped by the special features of those para-

1. I have not investigated the juristic literature of countries other than Germany, and so do not know what influence the notion may have had in jurisdictions other than the Federal Republic.
2. *Entscheidungen des Bundesgerichtshofes in Strafsachen* 1, 289.
3. Kern 1930, 338.
4. See the references in Hirsch 1967, 3 n. 8, 29 n. 40 and Tenckhoff 1974, 66 n. 18.
5. Hirsch 1967, 29–31.
6. Welzel 1969, 304. Hirsch was one of Welzel's students.
7. Tenckhoff 1974, 67.
8. Lenckner and others, 1982, 1180.
9. *Entscheidungen des Bundesgerichtshofes in Strafsachen* 36, 148.
10. For instance, Tenckhoff 1974, 66–67, 78–79.

graphs of the German penal code to which the notion of honor is relevant, and in any case do not seem to me sufficiently convincing to demand rebuttal here.

I have not attempted to trace in detail the history of the *Achtungsanspruch* theory before 1951, but my guess is that it is roughly as follows. The idea that a person has a right or a claim (*Anspruch*) to respect (*Achtung*) became prominent thanks to Kant.[11] Kant himself, in a discussion of defamation, brought this principle into close connection with the idea of honor.[12] Kant's ideas profoundly affected Anselm von Feuerbach, one of the most influential German writers on criminal law of the nineteenth century. Feuerbach began his discussion of offenses against honor as follows:

> *Respect* for a person is recognition of a value in him. If this respect is externally manifested, then the notion of *honor* comes into being [. . .] Respect itself is absolutely free and can never be the object of a legal claim; but to the extent that the external signs of respect can be brought within the purview of the law, a *right to honor* or *with respect to honor* is possible (Achtung *eines Menschen ist Anerkennung eines Werthes in ihm. Erscheint diese Achtung äusserlich, so entsteht der Begriff von Ehre [. . .] Die Achtung selbst ist unbedingt frei und kann nie Gegenstand rechtlicher Forderung sein; sofern aber die äusseren Zeichen der Achtung Rechtsgegenstand sein können, ist ein* Recht auf Ehre *oder in* Ansehung der Ehre *möglich*).[13]

Evidently, Feuerbach accepts Kant's idea that a person has a right to respect; and he says that a person has a legal right to the external manifestation of that respect, and that this manifestation is honor.

I presume that someone writing after Feuerbach made the shift from defining honor as the external manifestation of respect to defining it as the right to (the external manifestation of) respect. The first statement of this kind that I know of is by an obscure figure, Joseph Gabler, who in 1892 says that the task of criminal law is to defend the honor of a person, defined as "their right that the respect due to them should not be violated" (*Aufgabe des Strafrechts ist es [. . .] die Ehre der Person als ihren Anspruch auf Nichtverletzung der ihr*

11. "Every man has a legitimate claim to respect from his fellow men" (*ein jeder Mensch hat rechtmässigen Anspruch auf Achtung von seine Nebenmenschen*) Kant 1991, 255 = Ak. 462.
12. "Defamation [. . .] is contrary to the respect owed to humanity as such [. . .] The intentional *spreading* (*propalatio*) of something that detracts from another's honor [. . .] diminishes respect for humanity as such" (*Die üble Nachrede [. . .] ist der schuldigen Achtung gegen die Menschheit überhaupt zuwider [. . .] Die geflissentliche V e r b r e i t u n g* (propalatio) *desjenigen die Ehre eines anderen Schmälernden [. . .] ist Verringerung der Achtung für die Menschen überhaupt*) Kant 1991, 258 = Ak. 466.
13. Feuerbach 1847, 448. This is the fourteenth edition of the book; the first edition (which I have not seen) was published in 1801.

zukommenden Achtung zu schützen).[14] Gabler cites no authorities, but he also gives no indication that in saying this he considered himself to be putting forward an original idea. By 1951 the notion that honor is a right to respect had clearly been in the air, though never very prominent, for a long time.

I have read only a small fraction of the extensive German juristic literature on honor. In that small sample I have not seen anything resembling the arguments advanced in the present essay in defense of the notion of honor as a right.

14. Gabler 1892, 21.

APPENDIX TWO

Iceland

If people have a well-developed notion of honor then they will also have a sense of honor; but this is not a fact that will necessarily attract much attention. The modern Bedouin cannot often be caught referring to the sense of honor,[1] and the same is true of most medieval Europeans. But on the farthest fringe of medieval Europe there was probably an exception, and that is the Icelanders.[2]

What we know of their ideas on the subject of honor comes mainly from the sagas. In these works "the word *drengr* ['young man'] soon no longer has in view simply a (young) man, but rather—especially in the combination *góðr drengr* ['fine young man']—a particular male ideal, but one that (in contrast say to *mikilmenni* ['big man']) is in no way determined by external reputation, but solely by the inner value of the person in question."[3] Gehl glosses *drengr góðr*—this seems to be the more usual word order—as "'man of honor' (honor here meaning consciousness of honor)" (*„Ehrenmann" (Ehre hier gleich Ehrbewusstsein)*).[4] The phrase is a common one, and to be found in almost all the sagas.[5] Any free person could be a *drengr góðr*: not only a warrior, but equally a peasant or a trader;[6] and the phrase came to have a meaning so remote from its original sense that, as was mentioned in chapter 10, one could even say of a woman that she is a *drengr góðr*.[7]

The quality of being a *drengr góðr* is *drengskapr*, as it were 'drengliness', and this, in Gehl's view, generally means the honorableness that arises from the possession of a highly developed sense of honor.[8] Men who keep a pledge in

1. If I were called on to say to a Bedouin that so-and-so has a strong sense of honor, I would say '*arḍah* (or *wijhih*) *ġāliy lah* (or '*indih*) 'his honor is dear to him', and I believe this would be understood. I do not, however, know whether a Bedouin would say such a thing spontaneously.

2. Gehl 1937, 92–94 contrasts the Icelandic *drengskapr* 'sense of honor' with the concepts of knightly honor in the medieval literature of feudal Europe.

3. Gehl 1937, 84. The words between square brackets are not in the original.

4. Gehl 1937, 120. The author also translates *drengr góðr* as "a man who has a strong sense of honor" (*der Mann von Ehrgefühl*) (Gehl 1937, 113).

5. Gehl 1937, 92 n.

6. Gehl 1937, 92 n, 121.

7. Gehl 1937, 121.

8. Gehl usually translates *drengskapr* in the contexts that interest us as *Ehrenhaftigkeit* (see especially Gehl 1937, 100), but also as *anständige Gesinnung*, *ehrenhafte Gesinnung*, and *Edelmut*. He notes that occasionally it means no more than 'courage' (Gehl 1937, 84).

circumstances where the temptation to break it is strong thereby demonstrate *drengskapr*; when A and B have agreed to help each other in need, and A now needs B's help, A says that he expects the best from B's *drengskapr*; a woman conceals her son in her home from men who mean ill to him; when they arrive she lies to their leader, saying that the son would not avoid a meeting with him if he were at home, for she and her son trust the leader's *drengskapr*; and so on.[9]

Should we follow Gehl in translating *drengskapr*, in the relevant passages, as 'sense of honor' rather than, say, as 'nobility of character', 'sense of decency', 'integrity', 'fairness', or something of the sort? The answer to this depends on the answers to two further questions: first, whether the Icelanders had a concept of honor in the sense that interests us here, and second, if they did, whether the possession of *drengskapr* was something that gave one a title to honor.

It seems likely that the answer to both these further questions is yes. As regards the first, we find that Old Icelandic had a number of words—Gehl lists ten—that meant something like 'honor', 'standing', 'esteem', 'respect', or 'reputation', with one or two of them shading into 'fame' (for which there were also another half-dozen or more words).[10] Most of the honor words, apart from *drengskapr*, are generally used in an external way, but there are instances of some of them being used also in an internal sense.[11] The word *drengskapr* itself is almost always used to refer to a character trait, but there are also one or two occurrences where an external use seems to occur.[12] The two-sidedness of these words, which also appears in the fact that some occurrences are "equivocal,"[13] is a good indication that they do sometimes refer to a right.

The answer to the second question also seems to be positive. Gehl believed that the sagas showed the traces of a development from earlier and cruder notions of honor, which he groups under the heading of *forn siðr* ('ancient custom'), to the more refined ones that he called the spirit of *drengskapr*. The ideal under the *forn siðr* is the *mikilmenni*, the 'big man', who has distinguished ancestors, an affluent way of life, a dominating personality, and a leading position in society.[14] Under the spirit of *drengskapr*, in contrast, it is, as Gehl represents

9. These examples come from Gehl 1937, 85.

10. Gehl 1937, 30–31.

11. Gehl cites the following instances: "We would like to follow you, but it goes against my honor (*metnaðr*) to take part in this journey if I don't know its destination" (Gehl 1937, 26, 31, 158); "honor (*sómi*) demands that I do not abandon you while I am still alive" (Gehl 1937, 31; the translation is from Magnusson and Pálsson 1960, 242). Cf. Gehl 1937, 80–81.

12. Notably, where a man is said to lose his *drengskapr*: Gehl 1937, 85 (in the quotation from chapter 22 of the *Hávarðarsaga*), 122.

13. See the end of chapter 2 above.

14. Gehl 1937, 12–19.

it, the *drengr góðr* who has a title to honor, and what makes someone a *drengr góðr* is *drengskapr*, not social standing: Gehl talks of "the entirely classless aristocracy of the spirit of *drengskapr*."[15]

There remains a problem: Gehl says of all the honor words (apart from *drengskapr*) that "it is the world of ideas of the *forn siðr* and its concept of honor that are expressed in these words."[16] Are we to take it from this that a man who was recognized as a *drengr góðr* would not, for instance, thereby gain a title to *metnaðr* or *sœmð* (to mention two of the honor words)? If the answer to this is yes, then the idea that *drengskapr* gave a person a title to honor looks rather doubtful. I am proceeding, however, on the assumption that the answer is no.

I am not competent to judge the plausibility of Gehl's theory about the history of honor among the Icelanders, but it is at least evident that their ideas on the subject—whether or not they can be divided into two groups in the way that Gehl suggests—were complex and perhaps not wholly consistent. Gehl himself emphasizes this point.[17] It is also clear that the Icelanders placed far more emphasis on a person's moral virtues as giving a title to honor than people did in feudal Europe. The main emphasis of the sagas is on the conduct of the individual when faced with a challenge of some kind, above all something that can be viewed as a slight, and the spirit that a person shows in reacting to the challenge is the real test of honor. The sagas, in sharp contrast to the Arthurian romances of feudal Europe, allow a man to retain his honor even in defeat.[18] In all this the medieval Icelanders' notions are closer to those that developed elsewhere in Western Europe after the Renaissance than they are to the ideas of honor of their contemporaries in that region.

The imaginary example involving A and B in a homogeneous community that is given near the end of chapter 3 above was produced with Iceland in mind. Iceland was evidently a homogeneous community in the sense that there were no disagreements between groups as to the content of the honor code, even though there were considerable differences between individuals as to how they interpreted the code in their own lives.[19] In chapter 75 of *Njál's Saga*, two bothers, both honorable men, find themselves in the same situation, but deal with it in contrary ways.[20] But there is nothing in the story that assures

15. Gehl 1937, 13.
16. Gehl 1937, 80; similarly 31 n.
17. Gehl 1937, 22.
18. Thus, in chapter 85 of *Saint Óláf's Saga* in the *Heimskringla* we learn that King Hrœrek, deposed, blinded and exiled to Iceland by King Olaf of Norway, was nevertheless honored in his place of exile (Sturluson 1964, 330; Gehl 1937, 15).
19. Both these points are emphasized by Gehl (1937, 25, 47, 75).
20. See the analysis in Gehl 1937, 40–41.

us that either of them judged the other tolerantly, and indeed it sounds as if at least one of the two disapproved of the other's behavior.

I have concentrated here on the sense of honor, but the Icelandic material is also of great interest for other reasons, for instance, the interaction (which has still to be sorted out) between vertical honor of a highly competitive kind and horizontal honor.

BIBLIOGRAPHY

Abu-Lughod, Lila. 1986. *Veiled sentiments: Honor and poetry in a Bedouin society.* Berkeley: University of California Press.

Amelung, Knut. 1986. Das Hausfriedensbruch als Missachtung physisch gesicherter Territorialität. *Zeitschrift für die gesamte Strafrechtswissenschaft* 98:355–408.

Amira, Karl von. 1922. *Die germanische Todesstrafen.* Abhandlungen der bayerischen Akademie der Wissenschaften, philosophisch-philologische und historische Klasse, vol. 31, Abh. 3. Munich: Verlag der Bayerischen Akademie der Wissenschaften.

Angehrn, Otto. 1982. *Nachruf auf die Ehre.* Zurich: Schulthess.

Aristotle. 1926. *The "art" of rhetoric.* Ed. and trans. John Henry Freese. Loeb Classical Library, vol. 193. London: William Heinemann.

Asano-Tamanoi, Mariko. 1987. Shame, family, and state in Catalonia and Japan. In *Honor and shame and the unity of the Mediterranean,* ed. David Denny Gilmore, 104–20. A Special Publication of the American Anthropological Association, no. 22. Washington, D.C.: American Anthropological Association.

Bader-Weiss, G., and K. S. Bader. 1935. *Der Pranger.* Freiburg im Breisgau: Jos. Waibel.

Bailey, Clinton. 1991. How desert culture helps us understand the Bible: Bedouin law explains reaction to rape of Dinah. *Bible Review* 7 (August): 15–18, 20–21, 38.

al-Balāḏurī, Aḥmad b. Yaḥya. 1978. *Ansāb al-ašrāf,* vol. 3. Ed. 'A.-'A. Dūrī. Wiesbaden: Franz Steiner.

Barber, Charles Laurence. 1957. *The idea of honour in the English drama (1591–1700).* Gothenburg Studies in English, vol. 6. Gothenburg: n.p.

———. 1985. *The theme of honour's tongue: A study of social attitudes in the English drama from Shakespeare to Dryden.* Gothenburg Studies in English, vol. 58. Gothenburg: Acta Universitatis Gothoburgensis.

Bauman, Richard. 1986. Performance and honor in thirteenth-century Iceland. *Journal of American Folklore* 99:131–50.

Berdugo Gómez de la Torre, Ignacio. 1987. *Honor y libertad de expresión: las causas de justificación en los delitos contra el honor.* Madrid: Tecnos.

Berger, Adolf. 1953. Encyclopedic dictionary of Roman law. *Transactions of the American Philosophical Society* 43 (2): 333–808.

Berger, Peter. 1970. On the obsolescence of the concept of honor. *Archives européennes de sociologie* 11:339–47.

Berger, Peter L., Brigitte Berger, and Hansfried Kellner. 1973. *The homeless mind: Modernization and consciousness.* New York: Random House.

Beysterveldt, A. A. van. 1966. *Répercussions du souci de la pureté du sang sur la conception de l'honneur dans la «comedia nueva» espagnole.* Leiden: E. J. Brill.

Billacois, François. 1986. *Le duel dans la société française des XVIe–XVIIe siècles.* Civilisations et Sociétés, vol. 73. Paris: Éditions de l'École des Hautes Études en Sciences Sociales.

———. 1990. *The duel.* Ed. and trans. Trista Selous. New Haven and London: Yale University Press.

Binding, Karl. 1909. *Die Ehre. Der Zweikampf: zwei Vorträge.* Leipzig: Duncker und Humblot.

Bismarck, Otto von. 1929. *Die gesammelten Werke.* Vol. 12. Berlin: Otto Stollberg.

Blok, Anton. 1981. Rams and billy-goats: A key to the Mediterranean code of honour. *Man* 16:427–40.

Boehm, Christopher. 1987. *Blood revenge: The anthropology of feuding in Montenegro and other tribal societies.* 2d paperback ed., with expanded preface. Philadelphia: University of Pennsylvania Press.

Bollnow, Otto Friedrich. 1962. *Einfache Sittlichkeit: kleine philosophische Aufsätze.* 3d ed. Göttingen: Vandenhoeck und Ruprecht.

Bosl, Karl. 1977. Leitbilder und Wertvorstellungen des Adels von der Merowingerzeit bis zur Höhe der feudalen Gesellschaft. In *The epic in medieval society: Aesthetic and moral values,* ed. Harald Scholler, 18–36. Tübingen: Max Niemeyer.

Braine, John. 1968. *The crying game.* London: Eyre and Spottiswoode.

Brandes, Stanley. 1987. Reflections on honor and shame in the Mediterranean. In *Honor and shame and the unity of the Mediterranean,* ed. David Denny Gilmore, 121–34. A Special Publication of the American Anthropological Association, no. 22. Washington, D.C.: American Anthropological Association.

Brauer, Gerhard. 1930. *Das Ehrenwort im Vermögensrecht: eine rechtsgeschichtliche Untersuchung.* Doctoral Diss., University of Greifswald.

Brezina, Markus. 1987. *Ehre und Ehrenschutz im nationalsozialistischen Recht.* Augsburg: AV-Verlag.

Brückner, W. 1971–. Ehrenverpfändung. In *Handwörterbuch zur deutschen Rechtsgeschichte,* ed. Adalbert Erler and Ekkehard Kaufmann. Berlin: Erich Schmidt.

Bryson, Frederick Robertson. 1935. *The point of honor in sixteenth-century Italy: An aspect of the life of the gentleman.* Publications of the Institute of French Studies. New York: Columbia University.

———. 1938. *The sixteenth-century Italian duel: A study in Renaissance social history.* Chicago: University of Chicago Press.

Burckhardt, Jacob. 1989 [1860]. *Die Kultur der Renaissance in Italien.* Ed. Horst Günther. Frankfurt am Main: Deutscher Klassiker Verlag.

Burke, Peter. 1987. *The historical anthropology of early modern Italy.* Cambridge: Cambridge University Press.

Busquet, J. 1920. *Le droit de la vendetta et les paci corses.* Paris: A. Pedone.

Cachia, Pierre. 1989. *Popular narrative ballads of modern Egypt*. Oxford: Oxford University Press.

Cairns, Douglas L. 1993. *Aidōs: The psychology and ethics of honour and shame in ancient Greek literature*. Oxford: Clarendon Press.

Calderón de la Barca, Pedro. 1956. *Dramas de honor*. Vol. 1. *A secreto agravio, secreta venganza*. Ed. Angel Valbuena Briones. Clásicos Castellanos, vol. 141. Madrid: Espasa-Calpe.

————. 1961. *Four plays*. Trans. Edwin Honig. New York: Hill and Wang.

————. 1981. *El médico de su honra*. Ed. D. W. Cruickshank. Clásicos Castalia. Madrid: Editorial Castalia.

Campbell, J. K. 1966. Honour and the devil. In *Honour and shame: The values of Mediterranean society*, ed. J. G. Peristiany, 139–70. Chicago: University of Chicago Press.

Castro, Américo. 1956 [1916]. Algunas observaciones acerca del concepto del honor en los siglos XVI y XVII. In *Semblanzas y Estudios Españoles*, 319–82. Princeton: n.p.

Cavallo, Sandra, and Simona Cerutti. 1990. Female honor and the social control of reproduction in Piedmont between 1600 and 1800. In *Sex and gender in historical perspective*, ed. Edward Muir and Guido Ruggiero, 73–109. Baltimore and London: Johns Hopkins University Press.

Chauchadis, Claude. 1984. *Honneur morale et société dans l'Espagne de Philippe II*. Paris: Éditions du Centre National de la Recherche Scientifique.

Chrétien de Troyes. 1987. *Erec and Enide*. Ed. and trans. Carleton W. Carroll. Garland Library of Medieval Literature, Series A, vol. 25. New York: Garland Publishing.

————. 1991. *Arthurian romances*. Trans. William W. Kibler and Carleton W. Carroll. Harmondsworth: Penguin Books.

Christiansen, Hans. 1965. *Die Beleidigung: eine strafrechtlich-kriminologische Untersuchung unter besonderer Berücksichtigung der Fälle sozialtypischen Verhaltens, dargestellt an Hand der im Landgerichtsbezirk Kiel in den Jahren 1960–1962 durchgeführten Verfahren*. Doctoral Diss., University of Kiel.

Cohen, Elizabeth. 1992. Honor and gender in the streets of early modern Rome. *Journal of Interdisciplinary History* 22:597–625.

Cohen, Esther. 1993. *The crossroads of justice: Law and culture in late medieval France*. Leiden: E. J. Brill.

Collins, James. 1968. Honor. In *The world book encyclopedia*, vol. 9, 289. Chicago: Field Enterprises Educational Corporation.

Correa, Gustavo. 1958. El doble aspecto de la honra en el teatro del siglo XVII. *Hispanic Review* 26:99–107.

Dahm, Georg. 1931. *Das Strafrecht Italiens im ausgehenden Mittelalter: Untersuchungen über die Beziehungen zwischen Theorie und Praxis im Strafrecht des Spätmittelalters, namentlich im XIV. Jahrhundert*. Beiträge zur Geschichte der deutschen Strafrechtspflege, vol. 3. Berlin and Leipzig: Walter de Gruyter.

Davis, John. 1977. *People of the Mediterranean*. London: Routledge and
  Kegan Paul.
————. 1989. Col divorzio c'è differenza? In *Onore e storia nelle società medi-
  terranee*, ed. Giovanna Fiume, 47–59. Palermo: La Luna.
Deutsches Rechtswörterbuch. 1914–. Weimar: Hermann Böhlaus Nachfolger.
Douglas, William. 1887. *Duelling days in the army*. London: Ward and
  Downey.
Dresch, Paul. 1987. Placing the blame: A means of enforcing obligations in
  Upper Yemen. *Anthropos* 82: 427–43.
Dülmen, Richard van. 1990. *Theatre of horror: Crime and punishment in early
  modern Germany*. Trans. Elisabeth Neu. Cambridge: Polity Press.
Edgerton, Samuel Y. 1985. *Picture and punishment: Art and criminal prosecu-
  tion during the Florentine Renaissance*. Ithaca: Cornell University Press.
Erspamer, Francesco. 1982. *La biblioteca di don Ferrante: duello e onore nella
  cultura del cinquecento*. Rome: Bulzoni.
Farès, Bichr. 1932. *L'honneur chez les Arabes avant l'Islam*. Paris: Adrien-
  Maisonneuve.
Farr, James R. 1988. *Hands of honor: Artisans and their world in Dijon, 1550–
  1650*. Ithaca and London: Cornell University Press.
Feghali, Michel. 1938. *Proverbes et dictons syro-libanais*. Université de Paris,
  Travaux et Mémoires de l'Institut d'Ethnologie, vol. 31. Paris: Institut
  d'Ethnologie.
Fehr, Hans. 1908. *Der Zweikampf*. Berlin: Karl Curtius.
Ferrante, Lucia. 1990. Honor regained: Women in the Casa del Soccorso di
  San Paolo in sixteenth-century Bologna. In *Sex and gender in historical
  perspective*, ed. Edward Muir and Guido Ruggiero, 46–72. Baltimore
  and London: Johns Hopkins University Press.
Feuerbach, Paul Johann Anselm von. 1847. *Lehrbuch des gemeinen in
  Deutschland gültigen peinlichen Rechts*. Ed. C. J. A. Mittermaier. 14th
  ed. Giessen: George Friedrich Heyer.
Fielding, Henry. 1932 [1743]. *The life of Mr. Jonathan Wild the great*. The
  World's Classics, no. 382. London: Oxford University Press.
————. 1974 [1749]. *The history of Tom Jones a foundling*. 2 vols. Introduc-
  tion and commentary by Martin C. Battestin. Ed. Fredson Bowers.
  The Wesleyan Edition of the Works of Henry Fielding. Oxford:
  Clarendon Press.
————. 1983 [1751]. *Amelia*. Introduction and notes by Fredson Bowers.
  Ed. Martin C. Battestin. The Wesleyan Edition of the Works of Henry
  Fielding. Middleton, Conn.: Wesleyan University Press.
Finley, Moses I. 1977. *The world of Odysseus*. 2d ed. London: Chatto and
  Windus.
Fischer, Hubertus. 1983. *Ehre, Hof und Abenteuer in Hartmanns Iwein*. For-
  schungen zur Geschichte der älteren deutschen Literatur, vol. 3.
  Munich: Wilhelm Fink.
Fiume, Giovanna, ed. 1989. *Onore e storia nelle società mediterranee*. Pa-
  lermo: La Luna.
Fleskes, Paul. 1965. *Die Beleidigungskriminalität im Amtsgerichtsbezirk Ander-*

*nach am Rhein in den Jahren 1950–1960: eine kriminologische
Darstellung mit einer Einführung in die rechtliche Ausgestaltung der
Ehrverletzungsdelikte.* Inaugural-Diss. Rheinische Friedrich-Wilhelms-
Universität Bonn.

Flynn, Charles P. 1977. *Insult and society.* Port Washington, N.Y., and London: Kennikat Press.

Fontane, Theodor. 1967. *Effi Briest.* Trans. Douglas Parmée. Harmondsworth: Penguin Books.

Frevert, Ute. 1989. Die Ehre der Bürger im Spiegel ihrer Duelle: Ansichten
des 19. Jahrhunderts. *Historische Zeitschrift* 249:545–82.

————. 1991. *Ehrenmänner: das Duell in der bürgerlichen Gesellschaft.*
Munich: C. H. Beck.

Gabler, Joseph. 1892. *Das Vergehen der sogenannten üblen Nachrede (die Beleidigung des § 186 R.-St.-G.-R.).* Würzburg: H. Stürtz.

Garnsey, Peter. 1970. *Social status and legal privilege in the Roman Empire.*
Oxford: Clarendon Press.

Gautheron, Marie, ed. 1991a. Histoires de l'honneur et de la honte en CM1.
In *L'honneur: image de soi ou don de soi un idéal équivoque,* ed. Marie
Gautheron, 120–23. Paris: Éditions Autrement.

————. 1991b. *L'honneur: image de soi ou don de soi un idéal équivoque.*
Paris: Éditions Autrement.

Gauvard, Claude. 1991. *"De grace especial": crime, état et société en France à la
fin du moyen age.* 2 vols. Paris: Publications de la Sorbonne.

Gehl, Walther. 1937. *Ruhm und Ehre bei den Nordgermanen: Studien zum
Lebensgefühl der isländischen Saga.* Neue deutsche Forschungen, vol.
121. Berlin: Junker und Dünnhaupt.

Gernhuber, J. 1957. Strafvollzug und Unehrlichkeit. *Zeitschrift der Savigny-
Stiftung für Rechtsgeschichte, Germanistische Abteilung* 74:119–77.

Gesemann, Gerhard. 1943. *Heroische Lebensform.* Berlin: Wiking Verlag.

Gierke, Otto von. 1895–1917. *Deutsches Privatrecht.* 3 vols. Munich and
Leipzig: Duncker und Humblot.

Gilbert, Arthur N. 1976. Law and honour among eighteenth-century British
Army officers. *Historical Journal* 19:75–87.

Gilbert, Margaret. 1992 [1989]. *On social facts.* Princeton, N.J.: Princeton
University Press.

Gilmore, David D. 1982. Anthropology of the Mediterranean area. *Annual
Review of Anthropology* 11:175–205.

————, ed. 1987a. *Honor and shame and the unity of the Mediterranean.* A
Special Publication of the American Anthropological Association, no.
22. Washington, D.C.: American Anthropological Association.

————. 1987b. Introduction: The shame of dishonor. In *Honor and shame
and the unity of the Mediterranean,* ed. David Denny Gilmore, 2–21. A
Special Publication of the American Anthropological Association, no.
22. Washington, D.C.: American Anthropological Association.

————. 1990. On Mediterraneanist studies. *Current Anthropology* 31:395–96.

Greindl, M. 1940. Zum Ruhmes- und Ehrbegriff bei den Vorsokratikern.
Rheinisches Museum für Philologie, n.s., 89:216–28.

Hahn, Steven. 1984. Honor and patriarchy in the Old South. Review of Wyatt-Brown. *American Quarterly* 36:145–53.

Halkin, Léon-E. 1949. Pour une histoire de l'honneur. *Annales: Économies-Sociétés-Civilisations* 4:433–44.

Hart, H. L. A. 1982 [1973]. Legal rights. In *Essays on Bentham*, 162–93. Oxford: Clarendon Press.

Hartmann von Aue. 1984. *Iwein*. Ed. and trans. Patrick M. McConeghy. Garland Library of Medieval Literature, Series A, vol. 19. New York: Garland Publishing.

Helmholz, R. H., ed. 1985. *Select cases on defamation to 1600*. Publications of the Selden Society, vol. 101. London: Selden Society.

Herrmann, W. 1898. Ehre. In *Realencyklopädie für protestantische Theologie und Kirche*, ed. Albert Hauck, vol. 5, 227–29. Leipzig: J. C. Hinrich.

Herzfeld, Michael. 1980. Honour and shame: Problems in the comparative analysis of moral systems. *Man* 15:339–51.

————. 1985. *The poetics of manhood: Contest and identity in a Cretan mountain village*. Princeton, N.J.: Princeton University Press.

Heusler, Andreas. 1885–86. *Institutionen des deutschen Privatrechts*. 2 vols. Leipzig: Duncker und Humblot.

Hinds, Martin, and el-Said Badawi. 1986. *A dictionary of Egyptian Arabic*. Beirut: Librairie du Liban.

Hirsch, Hans. 1958 [1922]. *Die hohe Gerichtsbarkeit im deutschen Mittelalter*. Afterword by Theodor Mayer. 2d ed. Graz and Cologne: Hermann Böhlaus Nachfolger.

Hirsch, Hans Joachim. 1967. *Ehre und Beleidigung: Grundfragen des strafrechtlichen Ehrenschutzes*. Karlsruhe: C. F. Müller.

His, Rudolf. 1920–35. *Das Strafrecht des deutschen Mittelalters*. 2 vols. Weimar: Hermann Böhlaus Nachfolger.

Hu, Hsien Chin. 1944. The Chinese concept of face. *American Anthropologist* 46:45–64.

Hübner, Rudolf. 1930. *Grundzüge des deutschen Privatrechts*. 5th ed. Leipzig: A. Deichert.

Hupp, Otto. 1930. *Scheltbriefe und Schandbilder: ein Rechtsbehelf aus dem 15. und 16. Jahrhundert*. [Schleissheim]: Published by the author.

Ihering, Rudolph von. 1898. *Der Zweck im Recht*. 3d ed. 2 vols. Leipzig: Breitkopf und Härtel.

Jaussen, Antonin. 1948 [1908]. *Coutumes des Arabes au pays de Moab*. Paris: Adrien-Maisonneuve.

Jeudon, L. 1911. *La morale de l'honneur*. Paris: Librairie Félix Alcan.

Jones, George Fenwick. 1959. *Honor in German literature*. University of North Carolina Studies in the Germanic Languages and Literatures, no. 25. Chapel Hill: University of North Carolina Press.

Jouanna, Arlette. 1968. Recherches sur la notion d'honneur au XVIeme siècle. *Revue d'histoire moderne et contemporaine* 15:597–623.

Jowkar, Forouz. 1986. Honor and shame: A feminist view from within. *Feminist Issues* 6:45–65.

Kant, Immanuel. 1991. *The metaphysics of morals.* Introduction, translation, and notes by Mary Gregor. Cambridge: Cambridge University Press.

Kaser, Max. 1956. Infamia und ignominia in den römischen Rechtsquellen. *Zeitschrift der Savigny-Stiftung für Rechtsgeschichte, Romanistische Abteilung* 73:220–78.

Kelly, Fergus. 1988. *A guide to early Irish law.* Early Irish Law Series, vol. 3. Dublin: Dublin Institute for Advanced Studies.

Kelso, Ruth. 1929. *The doctrine of the English gentleman in the sixteenth century.* University of Illinois Studies in Language and Literature, vol. 14, nos. 1–2. Urbana, Ill: University of Illinois Press.

Kennan, George. 1891. *Siberia and the exile system.* 2 vols. New York: Century Co.

Kern, Eduard. 1930. Die Beleidigung. In *Festgabe für Reinhard von Frank zum 70. Geburtstag 16. August 1930: Beiträge zur Strafrechtswissenschaft,* ed. August Hegler, vol. 2, 335–64. Tübingen: J. C. B. Mohr.

Kettner, Robert Paul. 1890. *Der Ehrbegriff in den altfranzösischen Artusromanen: mit besonderer Berücksichtigung seines Verhältnisses zum Ehrbegriff in den altfranzösischen Chansons de geste.* Doctoral Diss. Leipzig: Fr. Richter.

Kisch, Guido. 1931. Ehrenschelte und Schandgemälde. *Zeitschrift der Savigny-Stiftung für Rechtsgeschichte, Germanistische Abteilung* 51:514–20.

————. 1980. *Ausgewählte Schriften.* Vol. 3. *Forschungen zur Rechts- und Sozialgeschichte des Mittelalters.* Sigmaringen: Jan Thorbecke.

Koch, Hans. 1972. *Zug.* Aarau: H. A. Bosch.

Kohler, Josef. 1900. Ehre und Beleidigung. *Archiv für Strafrecht und Strafprozess* 47:1–48, 98–154.

Korff, Wilhelm. 1966. *Ehre, Prestige, Gewissen.* Cologne: J. P. Bachem.

Kressel, Gideon M. 1981. Sororicide-filiacide—homicide for family honor. *Current Anthropology* 22:141–58.

————. 1988. More on honour and shame. *Man* 23:167–70.

————. 1992a. *Descent through males.* Mediterranean Language and Culture Monograph Series, vol. 8. Wiesbaden: Otto Harrassowitz.

————. 1992b. Shame and gender. *Anthropological Quarterly* 65:34–46.

Künssberg, Eberhard von. 1925. Rechtsgeschichte und Volkskunde. In *Die Volkskunde und ihre Grenzgebiete,* ed. Wilhelm Fraenger, 69–125. Jahrbuch für historische Volkskunde, vol. 1. Berlin: Herbert Stubenrauch.

————. 1930–31. Review of *Scheltbriefe und Schandbilder,* by Otto Hupp. *Zeitschrift für die Geschichte des Oberrheins* 44:601–2.

————. 1965 [1925]. *Rechtsgeschichte und Volkskunde.* Ed. Pavlos Tzermias. Rechtshistorische Arbeiten, vol. 3. Cologne: Böhlau Verlag.

Landi, Giulio. 1695 [1564]. *Delle azioni morali.* 2 vols. Piacenza: Gio. Bazachi.

Lenckner, Theodor, and others. 1982. *Strafgesetzbuch: Kommentar.* Original authors Adolf Schönke and Horst Schröder. 21st ed. Munich: C. H. Beck.

Lévy, Marie-Françoise; Anne Muxel; and Annick Percheron. 1991. Tableaux d'honneur. In *L'honneur: image de soi ou don de soi un idéal équivoque,* ed. Marie Gautheron, 104–19. Paris: Éditions Autrement.

Liebermann von Wahlendorf, Willy. 1988. *Erinnerungen eines deutschen Juden 1863–1936.* Munich and Zurich: Piper.

Liepmann, Moritz. 1906. Die Beleidigung. In *Vergleichende Darstellung des deutschen und ausländischen Strafrechts: Besonderer Teil,* by Karl Birkmeyer and others, vol. 4, 217–373. Berlin: Otto Liebmann.

———. 1909. *Die Beleidigung.* Berlin: Puttkammer und Mühlbrecht.

Liotta, Maurizio. 1980. Onore. In *Enciclopedia del diritto,* vol. 30, 202–9. Milan: Giuffrè.

Liszt, Franz von. 1908. *Lehrbuch des deutschen Strafrechts.* 16th and 17th eds. Berlin: J. Guttentag.

Livi, Giovanni. 1899. Il duello del Padre Cristoforo in relazione a documenti del tempo. *Nuova antologia di scienze, lettere ed arti* 165:738–43.

Lloyd-Jones, Hugh. 1990. Honour and shame in ancient Greek culture. In *Greek comedy, Hellenistic literature, Greek religion, and miscellanea,* 253–80. The academic papers of Sir Hugh Lloyd-Jones. Oxford: Clarendon Press.

Lünig, Johann Christian. 1713. *Das teutsche Reichs-archiv. Pars specialis.* Continuatio 3, Absatz 2. *Von der freyen Reichs-Ritterschaft in Francken.* Leipzig: Bey Friedrich Lanckischens Erben.

McKendrick, Melveena. 1984. Honour/vengeance in the Spanish 'comedia': A case of mimetic transference? *Modern Language Review* 79:313–35.

Mader, Hubert. 1983. *Duellwesen und altösterreichisches Offiziersethos.* Studien zur Militärgeschichte, Militärwissenschaft und Konfliktforschung, vol. 31. Osnabrück: Biblio Verlag.

Magnusson, Magnus, and Hermann Pálsson, trans. 1960. *Njal's saga.* Harmondsworth: Penguin Books.

Maitland, F. W., ed. 1974 [1889]. *Select pleas in manorial and other seignorial courts.* Publications of the Selden Society, vol. 2. London: Professional Books.

Maitland, F. W., and William Paley Baildon, eds. 1891. *The court baron: Being precedents for use in seignorial and other local courts together with select pleas from the bishop of Ely's court of Littleport.* Publications of the Selden Society, vol. 4. London: Bernard Quaritch.

Marston, Jerrilyn Greene. 1973. Gentry honour and royalism in early Stuart England. *Journal of British Studies* 13:21–43.

Martin, Ann G. 1984. *Shame and disgrace at King Arthur's court: A study in the meaning of ignominy in German Arthurian literature to 1300.* Göppinger Arbeiten zur Germanistik, no. 387. Göppingen: Kümmerle Verlag.

Martín Rodríguez, Jacinto. 1973. *El honor y la injuria en el Fuero de Vizcaya.* Bilbao: Diputación Provincial de Vizcaya.

Maurer, Friedrich. 1951. *Leid: Studien zur Bedeutungs- und Problemgeschichte besonders in den grossen Epen der staufischen Zeit.* Bern: A. Francke.

———. 1970 [1951]. Tugend und Ehre. In *Ritterliches Tugendsystem,* ed. Günter Eifler, 238–52. Darmstadt: Wissenschaftliche Buchgesellschaft.

Menéndez Pidal, Ramón, ed. 1955. *Primera crónica general de España*. 2d ed. 2 vols. Madrid: Gredos.

———. 1964 [1940]. Del honor en el teatro español. In *De Cervantes y Lope de Vega*. 6th ed., 145–73. Madrid: Espasa-Calpe.

Meulengracht Sørensen, Preben. 1983. *The unmanly man*. Odense: Odense University Press.

Mironov, V. 1991. *Duel v Rossii: zakony, nravi, obychai*. Moscow: Yuridicheskaya Literatura.

Mohrmann, R.-E. 1971–. Schmähen und Schelten. In *Handwörterbuch zur deutschen Rechtsgeschichte*, ed. Adalbert Erler and Ekkehard Kaufmann. Berlin: Erich Schmidt.

Mommsen, Theodor. 1899. *Römisches Strafrecht*. Systematische Handbuch der Rechtswissenschaft. Leipzig: Duncker und Humblot.

Montaigne, Michel de. 1958. *The complete essays*. Trans. Donald M. Frame. Stanford: Stanford University Press.

Morel, Henri. 1964. La fin du duel judiciaire en France et la naissance du point d'honneur. *Revue historique de droit français et étranger*, 4th series, 42:574–639.

Morris, Christopher. 1966 [1955]. *The Tudors*. N.p.: Fontana Collins.

Muchembled, Robert. 1991. Les humbles aussi. In *L'honneur: image de soi ou don de soi un idéal équivoque*, ed. Marie Gautheron, 61–68. Paris: Éditions Autrement.

Muhawi, Ibrahim. 1989. L'ideale onorifico nella società palestinese tradizionale. In *Onore e storia nelle società mediterranee*, ed. Giovanna Fiume, 263–86. Palermo: La Luna.

Musco, Enzo. 1974. *Bene giuridico e tutela dell'onore*. Raccolta di studi di diritto penale, vol. 20. Milan: A Giuffrè.

Naendrup, Hubert. 1905. Dogmengeschichte der Arten mittelalterlicher Ehrenminderungen. In *Festgabe für Felix Dahn*, vol. 1, 221–382. Breslau: M. und H. Marcus.

Neuschel, Kristen B. 1989. *Word of honor: Interpreting noble culture in sixteenth-century France*. Ithaca and London: Cornell University Press.

Nordenstam, Tore. 1968. *Sudanese ethics*. Uppsala: Scandinavian Institute of African Studies.

Nörr, Dieter. 1989. *Aspekte des römischen Völkerrechts: die Bronzetafel von Alcántara*. Bayrische Akademie der Wissenschaften, Philosophisch-Historische Klasse, Abhandlungen, Neue Folge, vol. 101. Munich: Bayrische Akademie der Wissenschaften.

O'Leary, Philip. 1987. The honour of women in early Irish literature. *Ériu* 38:27–44.

Oppermann, Hans. 1983 [1967]. Vorbemerkung. In *Römische Wertbegriffe*, ed. Hans Oppermann. Darmstadt: Wissenschaftliche Buchgesellschaft.

Orlandis [Rovira], José. 1944. La paz de la casa en el derecho español de la alta edad media. *Anuario de historia del derecho español* 15:107–61.

Ortalli, Gherardo. 1979. « . . . *pingatur in Palatio* . . . »: *la pittura infamante nei secoli XIII–XVI*. Rome: Jouvence.

Bibliography

Osenbrüggen, Eduard. 1857. *Der Hausfrieden: ein Beitrag zur deutschen Rechtsgeschichte*. Erlangen: Ferdinand Enke.

―――. 1969 [1868]. *Studien zur deutschen und schweizerischen Rechtsgeschichte*. Aalen: Scientia Verlag.

Pappas, John. 1982. La campagne des philosophes contre l'honneur. *Studies on Voltaire and the Eighteenth Century* 205:31–44.

Patterson, Orlando. 1982. *Slavery and social death*. Cambridge, Mass.: Harvard University Press.

Peristiany, J. G., ed. 1966 [1965]. *Honour and shame: The values of Mediterranean society*. Chicago: University of Chicago Press.

Peristiany, J. G., and Julian Pitt-Rivers, eds. 1991a. *Honour and grace in Mediterranean society*. Cambridge: Cambridge University Press.

―――. 1991b. Introduction. In *Honour and grace in Mediterranean society*, ed. J. G. Peristiany and Julian Pitt-Rivers, 1–17. Cambridge: Cambridge University Press.

Peters, Edward. 1990. Wounded names: The medieval doctrine of infamy. In *Law in mediaeval life and thought*, ed. Edward B. King and Susan J. Ridyard. *Sewanee Medieval Studies* 5:43–89. Sewanee, Tenn.: Press of the University of the South.

Pina-Cabral, João de. 1989. The Mediterranean as a category of regional comparison: A critical view. *Current Anthropology* 30:399–406.

Pitarch, José Luis, ed. 1984. *El honor y el honor militar*. Barcelona: Grijalbo.

Pitt-Rivers, Julian. 1966. Honour and social status. In *Honour and shame: The values of Mediterranean society*, ed. J. G. Peristiany, 19–77. Chicago: University of Chicago Press.

―――. 1968. Honor. In *International encyclopedia of the social sciences*, ed. David Sills, vol. 6, 503–11. N.p.: Macmillan, Free Press.

―――. 1977. *The fate of Shechem*. Cambridge Studies in Social Anthropology, no. 19. Cambridge: Cambridge University Press.

―――. 1991. La maladie de l'honneur. In *L'honneur: image de soi ou don de soi un idéal équivoque*, ed. Marie Gautheron, 20–36. Paris: Éditions Autrement.

Plucknett, Theodore F. T. 1956. *A concise history of the common law*. 5th ed. Boston: Little, Brown.

Pólay, Elémer. 1989. Der Schutz der Ehre und des guten Rufes im römischen Recht. *Zeitschrift der Savigny-Stiftung für Rechtsgeschichte, Romanistische Abteilung* 106:502–34.

Possevino, Giovanni Battista. 1553. *Dialogo dell'honore*. Venice: Gabriel Giolito de Ferrari e Fratelli.

Postgate, R. W. 1929. *That devil Wilkes*. New York: Vanguard Press.

Reiner, Hans. 1956. *Die Ehre: kritische Sichtung einer abendländischen Lebens- und Sittlichkeitsform*. Darmstadt: E. S. Mittler und Sohn.

Riedinger, Jean-Claude. 1976. Remarques sur la timé chez Homère. *Revue des Études Grecques* 89:244–64.

Riezler, Erwin. 1929. Ehre. In *Rechtsvergleichendes Handwörterbuch für das Zivil- und Handelsrecht des In- und Auslandes*, ed. Franz Schlegelberger, vol. 2, 758–72. Berlin: Franz Vahlen.

Bibliography

Rivanera, Jose. J. 1961 [1954]. *Código de honor comentado*. Biblioteca del Oficial, vol. 508. Buenos Aires: Círculo Militar Argentino.

Robreau, Yvonne. 1981. *L'honneur et la honte: leur expression dans les romans en prose du Lancelot-Graal (XIIe–XIIIe siècles)*. Publications Romanes et Françaises, vol. 157. Geneva: Librairie Droz.

Roosevelt, Archie. 1988. *For lust of knowing: Memoirs of an intelligence officer*. Boston and Toronto: Little, Brown.

Rundstein, S. 1905. Aechtungs- und Schmähungsklausel im polnischen Obligationenrechte des Mittelalters. *Zeitschrift für vergleichende Rechtswissenschaft* 17:23–34.

Saikaku, Ihara. 1981. *Tales of Samurai honor: Buke Giri Monogatari*. Trans. Caryl Ann Callahan. Tokyo: Monumenta Nipponica, Sophia University.

Saitō, Shōji. 1983. Honor. In *Kodansha Encyclopedia of Japan*, vol. 3, 224. Tokyo: Kodansha.

Salvioli, Giuseppe. 1892. La casa e la sua inviolabilità in Italia dopo il secolo XIII secondo gli statuti e la giurisprudenza. In *Per il XXXV anno d'insegnamento di Filippo Serafini: studi giuridici*, by Enrico Bensa and others, 389–402. Florence: Barbèra.

Schneider, Jane. 1971. Of vigilance and virgins: Honor, shame and access to resources in Mediterranean societies. *Ethnology* 10:1–24.

Schopenhauer, Arthur, n.d. [1851]. *Aphorismen zur Lebensweisheit*. Ed. Arthur Hübscher and Hans Lankes. N.p.: Goldmann.

Seneca. 1935. *Moral essays*. Ed. and trans. John W. Basore. Vol. 1. *De constantia*, 48–105. Loeb Classical Library, vol. 214. Cambridge, Mass.: Harvard University Press.

Serrano Martínez, Encarnación Irene. 1956. *"Honneur" y "honor": su significación a través de la literatura francesa y española (desde los orígenes hasta el siglo XVI)*. Murcia: Universidad de Murcia.

Serra Ruiz, Rafael. 1969. *Honor, honra e injuria en el derecho medieval español*. Murcia: Sucesores de Nogués.

Settegast, Franz. 1885. Der Ehrbegriff im altfranzösischen Rolandsliede. *Zeitschrift für romanische Philologie* 9:204–22.

———. 1887. *Die Ehre in den Liedern des Troubadours*. Leipzig: Veit.

Shakespeare, William. 1969. *Troilus and Cressida*. Ed. Alice Walker. Cambridge: Cambridge University Press.

———. 1975. *Twelfth night*. Ed. J. M. Lothian and T. W. Craik. The Arden Shakespeare. London: Methuen.

Sharpe, J. A. n.d. *Defamation and sexual slander in early modern England: The church courts at York*. Borthwick Papers, vol. 58. York: Borthwick Institute of Historical Research, University of York.

Siegel, Heinrich. 1894. *Der Handschlag und Eid nebst den verwandten Sicherheiten für ein Versprechen im deutschen Rechtsleben*. Sitzungsberichte der philosophisch-historischen Classe der kaiserlichen Akademie der Wissenschaften, vol. 130, no. 6. Vienna: F. Tempsky.

Simpson, A. W. B. 1986. *A history of the land law*. 2d ed. Oxford: Clarendon Press.

Simson, Gerhard, and Friedrich Geerds. 1969. *Straftaten gegen die Person und Sittlichkeitsdelikte in rechtsvergleichender Sicht.* Munich: C. H. Beck.

Squibb, George Drewry. 1959. *The high court of chivalry: A study of the civil law in England.* Oxford: Clarendon Press.

Steul, Willi. 1981. *Paschtunwali: ein Ehrenkodex und seine rechtliche Relevanz.* Beiträge zur Südasienforschung, Südasien-Institut, Universität Heidelberg, vol. 54. Wiesbaden: Franz Steiner.

Stewart, Frank H. 1986. *Bedouin boundaries in central Sinai and the southern Negev.* Mediterranean Language and Culture Monograph Series, no. 2. Wiesbaden: Otto Harrassowitz.

————. 1987a. A Bedouin narrative from central Sinai. *Zeitschrift für arabische Linguistik* 16:44–92.

————. 1987b. Tribal law in the Arab world: A review of the literature. *International Journal of Middle East Studies* 19:473–90.

————. 1988–90. *Texts in Sinai Bedouin law.* 2 vols. Mediterranean Language and Culture Monograph Series, no. 5. Wiesbaden: Otto Harrassowitz.

————. 1990. Schuld and Haftung in Bedouin law. *Zeitschrift der Savigny-Stiftung für Rechtsgeschichte, Germanistische Abteilung* 107:393–407.

————. 1991. The woman, her husband and her guardian in the law of the Sinai Bedouin. *Arabica* 38:102–29.

Stone, Lawrence. 1990. *Road to divorce: England 1530–1987.* Oxford: Oxford University Press.

Sturluson, Snorri. 1964. Heimskringla: *History of the kings of Norway.* Trans. Lee M. Hollander. Austin: University of Texas Press.

Summer, L. W. 1987. *The moral foundation of rights.* Oxford: Clarendon Press.

Tackmann, S. 1975. Die moralische Begriffe Ehre und Würde in der sowjetischen Ethikliteratur. *Deutsche Zeitschrift für Philosophie* 23:172–77.

Taylor, Gabriele. 1985. *Pride, shame and guilt: Emotions of self-assessment.* Oxford: Clarendon Press.

Tenckhoff, Jörg. 1974. *Die Bedeutung des Ehrbegriffs für die Systematik der Beleidigungstatbestände.* Strafrechtliche Abhandlungen, n.s., 21. Berlin: Duncker und Humblot.

Terraillon, Eugène. 1912. *L'honneur: sentiment et principe moral.* Paris: Librairie Félix Alcan.

Thielicke, Helmut. 1982. Ehre. In *Theologische Realenzyklopädie,* ed. Gerhard Krause and Gerhard Müller, vol. 9, 362–66. Berlin: Walter de Gruyter.

Trabandt, Joachim. 1970. *Der kriminalrechtliche Schutz des Hausfriedens in seiner geschichtlichen Entwicklung.* Doctoral Diss., University of Hamburg.

Treggiari, Susan. 1991. *Roman marriage.* Oxford: Clarendon Press.

Ulf, Christoph. 1990. *Die homerische Gesellschaft.* Munich: C. H. Beck.

Vermeyden, Paula. 1990. Eer en aanzien in twee ijslandse saga's. *Amsterdamer Beiträge zur älteren Germanistik* 30:93–109.

Vescovi, Vincenzo. 1902–6. Ingiuria e diffamazione. In *Il digesto italiano,* ed. Luigi Lucchini, vol. 13, pt. 1. Turin: Unione Tipografico.

Villey, Michel. 1964. La genèse du droit subjectif chez Guillaume d'Occam. *Archives de philosophie du droit* 9:97–127.

Vocabularium iurisprudentiae romanae. 1894–. Berlin: Walter de Gruyter.

Wambaugh, Joseph. 1986. *The secrets of Harry Bright.* Toronto: Bantam Books.

Watson, Alan. 1963. Some cases of distortion by the past in classical Roman law. *Tijdschrift voor rechtsgeschiedenis—Revue d'histoire du droit* 31:69–91.

———. ed. 1985. *The Digest of Justinian.* Philadelphia: University of Pennsylvania Press.

Watson, Curtis Brown. 1960. *Shakespeare and the Renaissance concept of honor.* Princeton: Princeton University Press.

Weber, Adolph Dietrich. 1793–94. *Über Iniurien und Schmähschriften.* 1st ed. 2 vols. Schwerin and Wismar: In der Boednerischen Buchhandlung.

Weinrich, Harald. 1971. Mythologie der Ehre. In *Terror und Spiel,* ed. Manfred Fuhrmann, 341–56. Munich: Wilhelm Fink.

Welzel, Hans. 1969. *Das deutsche Strafrecht.* 11th ed. Berlin: Walter de Gruyter.

Westermarck, Edward. 1912–17. *The origin and development of moral ideas.* 2d ed. 2 vols. London: Macmillan.

White, Alan R. 1984. *Rights.* Oxford: Clarendon Press.

Wikan, Unni. 1984. Shame and honour: A contestable pair. *Man* 19:635–52.

Wilson, Edward M. 1953. Family honour in the plays of Shakespeare's predecessors and contemporaries. In *Essays and Studies, 1953,* ed. Geoffrey Bullough, 19–40. Essays and Studies Collected for the English Association. London: John Murray.

Wittmann, Roland. 1974. Die Entwicklungslinien der klassischen Injurienklage. *Zeitschrift der Savigny-Stiftung für Rechtsgeschichte, Romanistische Abteilung* 91:285–59.

Wyatt-Brown, Bertram. 1982. *Southern honor: Ethics and behavior in the old South.* New York and Oxford: Oxford University Press.

al-Yaʿqūbī, Aḥmad b. Abī Yaʿqūb. 1883. *Taʾrīx.* Ed. M. Th. Houtsma. 2 vols. Leiden: E. J. Brill.

Yavetz, Zvi. 1974. *Existimatio, fama* and the Ides of March. *Harvard Studies in Classical Philology* 78:35–65.

Zuckermann-Ingber, Alix. 1984. *El bien más alto: A reconsideration of Lope da Vega's honor plays.* Gainesville: University Presses of Florida.

Zunkel, Friedrich. 1975. Ehre, Reputation. In *Geschichtliche Grundbegriffe: historisches Lexikon zur politisch-sozialen Sprache in Deutschland,* ed. Otto Brunner, Werner Conze, and Reinhart Koselleck, vol. 2, 1–63. Stuttgart: Ernst Klett.

INDEX